LIGHTING
THE
PATH

LIGHTING THE PATH

Leaning into a Hopeful Future
as a Special Needs Parent

Marcia Nathai-Balkissoon

Lighting the Path
Leaning into a Hopeful Future as a Special Needs Parent

Copyright © 2021 by Marcia Nathai-Balkissoon

All rights reserved. No part of this book may be reproduced or transmitted in any form or by any means without written permission of the author.

Cover design: MiblArt
Interior formatting: Alt 19 Creative

ISBNs:
978-1-950476-21-3 (paperback)
978-950476-23-7 (eBook)
978-1-950476-24-4 (hardcover)

Published by:

*To Uncle Frank who,
without me understanding it mattered,
taught me about the resilience of
special needs people in all he did.*

Contents

Preface		1
1	Acknowledging What Happened	9
2	Coping with the Situation Today	21
3	Managing Aloneness and Isolation	33
4	Clarifying Your Powerful Vision	47
5	Exploring Spiritual Elements of This Journey	59
6	Shaping At-Home Interventions	71
7	Supporting Your Other Children	97
8	Bolstering Your Love Relationship	115
9	Boosting Your Health	131
10	Improving Your Financial Situation	147
11	Celebrating Your Resilience	163
Epilogue		175
Appendix A		177
Appendix B		181
Acknowledgments		187
About the Author		189

Preface

Emma's birth

"You're being irresponsible to expect your daughter to have any chance at recovery. If she lives, Emma will remain in a vegetative state into adulthood," said the doctor, and I heard matter-of-fact finality in his tone. Some observer part of me dispassionately kept me on my feet, speaking to Sean, my husband, and blinking, laughing and playing with Bryan, our five-year-old son, there in the Intensive Care Unit. I did not hurl insults, my fists, or even blame, although our world was crashing down around us.

Had I been watching this in a movie, I'd have been horrified, drawn to tears from feeling the pain of another mother and watching her baby's future just crash in an instant. But this was my real life, and some supernatural force or innate ability was keeping my family upright. Observing Emma comatose in the hospital bed, all I could do was hold close my memory of the eight months we'd had with her so far. If what the doctors were saying came true, we were likely at the end of the line.

> *This was my real life, and some supernatural force or innate ability was keeping my family upright.*

Emma was born in 2012. At the ultrasound when her health was checked, I remember specifically answering the call of my intuition and asking for a check of her fingers and toes. All was well, we were told. Other than having a huge pregnancy belly, I'd had an easy pregnancy. Em hadn't been a rib-kicker like my son had been five years earlier, and what a relief that was! So, it was a surprise when Emma was born with six fingers on one hand. Feeling woozy, I thought the drugs were causing me to count wrong, and I recounted, holding her precious little fingers, so gently, and came up with six again. I called my husband over to count and he started to cry.

A biology teacher, he explained that this simple polydactyly (having extra fingers) could be an indicator of organ malformation issues in our precious newborn. Given that the medical team present for the birth had not clued us in to any observed anomalies with her fingers, he requested the paediatric neurologist to specifically check her out based on his concerns. The next day started with a solemn visit from that doctor. He confirmed that Emma did in fact have a moderate-to-large hole in her heart, based on the whooshing sound heard through his stethoscope.

We were referred to a paediatric cardiologist, then, and when Em was 18 days old, learned that she actually had four issues in her heart—a critical congenital heart defect called Tetralogy of Fallot that included an aortic valve anomaly, a hole between the two lower heart chambers, stenosis (constriction) of the pulmonary artery, which would make it hard to get enough oxygen-rich blood to Emma's body, and a thickened right ventricle wall.

Were we living in a first-world country, the problem would likely have been fixed through surgery immediately, but living in Trinidad and Tobago, there were no surgical options. We were told that any such surgery happened through the work of rarely-visiting teams or through scheduling of surgery in a foreign country. Worse, we were told we had to wait until Emma's condition declined to a point where it made intervention mandatory. Throughout the coming months, the doctor's prognosis hung over our heads like the Sword of Damocles.

When Emma was eight months old, her condition suddenly worsened when she turned blue in her crib. We learned she was at high risk for stroke or seizure without immediate open-heart surgery. A U.S. hospital agreed to help Emma, and a week later, payments and pre-tests were being sorted out.

The day before Emma's surgery, she was pushing up to stand and reaching to pull at the doodads on an activity centre. Seeing that for the first time, we were so thrilled! We could not wait to have this heart issue repaired and continue with the beautiful and active life we were sure she was destined to live.

Surgery was carded to start at 7 a.m. the next day, and we handed Emma over to the male nurse outside of the theatre door. We took a picture of our little family, kissed her good luck, and listened to the nurse promising to take good care of our girl. When we were finally allowed to see Em, she was in an ICU bed, and we were told that the surgery had been successful. Since her breathing was strong and steady, the doctors decided to take her off ventilator that very night. They said she would recover even faster with the tube out of her throat.

I am still incredulous about what happened next. Somehow, while removing her ventilation tube, the doctor dislodged a tube from Emma's heart, and she began bleeding out. Sean and I observed the box at the foot of her bed filling with blood and called the nurse's attention to it. Emma flatlined (i.e., her heart stopped) for twenty minutes that night. Several units of blood and a huge team could not help her. Sean and I listened to the chaos and felt powerless. I did not consider myself a strongly religious person, but with nowhere left to turn, we held hands and prayed. "Lord," I remember saying, "I know I have always prayed for you to help me accept your will, but I can't anymore. Please give us back our child." Immediately, Emma's heart restarted.

Emma flatlined for twenty minutes that night.

In an effort to support her survival and recovery, doctors lowered Emma's body temperature, inducing a state of hypothermia to reduce her chances of organ failure. The doctors expected her organs to shut down; they did not. She was being given a total food intake of 5ml of my breastmilk per day via a nasogastric tube, and her digestive system tolerated that, thankfully. When two weeks passed with Emma seeming to be still in a coma, an MRI was done. On it, instead of her brain appearing grey, it was fully white, and the doctors reported to us that her brain had been "wiped", causing the loss of all five of her senses, as well as her ability to suck and swallow. Their prognosis was that Emma would be in a vegetative state for the rest of her life.

Several doctors and nurses cried. I think we vacillated between a feeling that reality had been suspended and one that all hope was lost. With our son Bryan right there with us, we cried in secret. We kept trying to function normally for his sake, and just in case Em could hear us. In addition to hearing that it was irresponsible to expect recovery for Em, we also were encouraged to "let her go" and move on with our lives.

But how could we have prayed for her to come back to us and then decided it was inconvenient to keep her in our life? With a dark future looming, we had decisions to make, and our first was that we absolutely wanted our girl! Whatever lay ahead, she was our gift and we felt so heart-full to have her back with us, even with the heartbreak we were also feeling. This made the second decision automatic: to risk surgery to have Emma fitted with a gastrostomy tube so we could feed her more milk and begin rebuilding her body size which had drastically shrunk. Third, we decided to put all our focus and energy into enhancing Em's chances of recovery, by reading, researching, doing courses, getting her into rehab and therapy programs, and each of us fulfilling roles to support her in our day to day lives.

Emma today

Today, Emma is nine years old. We have been back home with her for over eight years. The hospital allowed us to take her to rehab for a few weeks during which we avidly observed what was being done by physical, occupational and speech therapists while she was semi-comatose. There, Emma made progress, but she left in a slightly better state than she had entered.

Emma has been through the wringer, but she has borne the pain and the confusion with such aplomb and joy that we are regularly inspired by her attitude. She has had scores of medical visits, including paediatrics, paediatric neurology, developmental paediatrics, paediatric cardiology, orthopaedics, osteopathy, and surgery. Some doctors have been compassionate and competent, and others have seemed heartless and mercenary. We have taken her to various alternative, physical, occupational, speech, and early intervention therapy visits.

At this point, Emma is considered a child with multiple disabilities. She has severe traumatic brain injury, a mild to moderate pulmonary backflow following the open-heart surgery, a blind diagnosis, difficulty sucking and swallowing and chewing, an inability to speak, immobility, challenges with gut motility, hernias in her chest wall and abdomen, hypertonic (stretched out, rigid) limbs and hypotonic (floppy) neck and torso, some positional scoliosis (excessive curving of her spine), and some loss of muscle tone especially in her legs. The tightness of her legs causes scissoring, and this has caused double dislocation of her hips. Em also has poor circulation as she cannot move her limbs easily, and so her hands and feet become cold and purple if we don't get them moving or propped up to encourage flow back to her heart.

Our little fighter has also overcome many limitations to date. Her gastrostomy tube has been removed and she has been able to transition from eating watery purées to eating crushed food and taking bites of soft fruit. Not only has she regained her hearing, but she has favourite songs spanning nursery rhymes, prayers, Christmas, pop, classical, soul, calypso, and R&B music. Em can make a few sounds that approximate words (dada, hello, ah-la-la [I love you], and ah-tee [aunty]) and is just beginning to vocalise at certain points in songs. She lifts her hand to show she wants another mouthful, or another kiss, and she is learning to move her hand to locate a tower of blocks and knock it down. Where once even the slightest touch caused her pain, she now derives comfort and joy from both light touch and deep pressure massage. Her latest joy is dry brushing, which we do to improve circulation in her limbs. Em is kicking her legs some more recently, when she gets excited about a song that she likes, and that has the potential to improve muscle tone and circulation to an extent.

My intention with this book

When Emma was hurt, I remember how lost and scared and lonely we felt. We wanted guidance, advice, and assurance that it would be okay. We wanted to talk to others who had faced this before. I had done searches of online bookstores and bought a book about brain injury. But that was so distant and professional; I really longed for some love and human connection too.

That is why I am writing this book. I don't want another parent or guardian to ever have to face what we did alone. This book was written for every person who feels fear about something that has just happened to a loved one. In the moment Sean and I faced Emma's prognosis, it felt like we'd been slammed by a tsunami of emotion and overwhelm. We were ill-equipped and facing a storm of grief for our little girl, at the same time. What we needed at that moment was someone else who understood. Perhaps you feel as though a raging flood has swept you off your feet too. This book is especially for parents and guardians of children with special needs, whether those children have been born with special needs or, like Emma, suffered through an event that caused or exacerbated those special needs.

> When Emma was hurt, I remember how lost and scared and lonely we felt.

My wish is that this book gives you the comfort of knowing you are not alone. Others, including us, have walked the path too, and I want to share some of our experiences and takeaways and hope with you. I'll share some of the emotional journeys we have traversed, recount how we dealt with them, and recommend some exercises that could be of use to you and your family. Dealing with feelings of being judged by others, blaming ourselves, feeling abandoned and isolated, feeling angry and overwhelmed and hopeless are just some of the negative emotions explored in the chapters ahead.

A big part of the worry for us was focused on finding ways in which we could help our child to recover, despite her medical prognosis. Thus, this book also outlines several of the approaches we have used, from traditional medicine and therapy to intuition-based approaches used at home and reviewed from time to time with various practitioners.

If you have a significant other or other children then it is likely that you are juggling added expectations related to those relationships. I've found managing these relationships have been critical and also extremely challenging, so I've touched on these issues in separate chapters too.

For several years, I have lived with a dark cloud of fear hovering over me. I worried about how to provide financially for my family and especially for Em, not only now but even more scary, when Sean and I have passed on. This is a big concern for me still, and I've put a lot of thought and research into how to chart our financial course. So, the financial planning chapter sheds some light on options you should explore to put things in place for your special needs child and other children, for your own retirement, and more. The issue of career comes up also, because our work generates the income to keep caring for our families. You can check out some content to help you balance work demands and do some personal planning, as well.

Speaking about wealth, you may have heard the saying "your health is your wealth". I've included a chapter on focusing on your own health because we need to stay healthy and build our strength and longevity for our children's sakes. Also, of course you boost your family's wellbeing when you learn about eating and living for health.

I do have to say that nothing I write should be construed as legal or medical advice, but I hope it feels like you have the warm hand of a friend holding yours as you navigate your journey. I know how difficult, never-ending, and lonely this can feel, my friend. I truly hope that through my words you feel less alone and more resilient and hopeful.

CHAPTER 1

Acknowledging What Happened

FOR YEARS, NOT just months, after Emma was incapacitated, I remember feeling like I'd been flattened by a hurricane, and that hurricane had washed away most of the landmarks in my life: most of our friends and family, most of our finances, and most of our happiness and hope. When I looked for hope by reading uplifting quotes, I would come across wisdom that sounded like this one:

> *Don't be the reason you're unhappy or not successful. If you don't know what's happening in life, make a change."* Elle Sommer

What filled me was a pungent rage, borne of the feeling that life was being so unfairly nasty to me. Was this person dispensing a platitude that relegated my struggle to mindset rather than a series of unfortunate

> I remember feeling like I'd been flattened by a hurricane, and that hurricane had washed away most of the landmarks in my life.

events, and daring to suggest that if I just changed myself, I'd be happy again? Yeah, my mental shift was a magic wand to undo the mistake that had turned all our lives into a lifetime of pressure, worry and fear. Instead of feeling empowered, I felt so empty and broken as I read quotes about happiness and the need to see the obstacle as the way.

The truth was that I didn't believe I could be honest about how I felt. I decided my family depended on me and so I had to be strong. With Sean's support, I had to figure out how to start seeing more positivity, even while realistically facing the lifelong challenges we would be navigating as a family.

As I look back and write this chapter these are the questions I ask myself:

1. Was I *genuinely* being strong as I put one foot in front of the other each day for years?
   or
2. Was I only *pretending* to be strong?

To answer that, I believe I was doing both things simultaneously. I kept on living as we all must, come what may, and doing it because I needed to make an income to afford therapy and medical care for Emma in addition to the regular expenses of our life. I was also experiencing the strain, with a child who no longer slept at all during the day. Emma only slept for perhaps four interrupted hours each night, preferring to laugh and sing with me even at 3 a.m. and waiting for her daddy to feed her and sleep beside her (all of which still remains true eight years later).

My husband stalwartly slept beside Emma almost every night. He never complained and he never wanted to leave her side. He said to me once that we did not know how long she would be with us, and if anything ever happened, he wanted to know he had done all he could for her. I watched the physical, mental, and emotional strain take a toll on him. He endured headaches and we both suffered lower back pain. His once youthful face seemed to age in fast-forward. My heart broke watching the shift happen so rapidly.

Shortly after we returned home with Emma in her semi-comatose state, Sean and I talked about trying to balance challenges at work. I shifted my work hours to evenings and nights, in order to be able to keep my job and see to Em's medical and therapy needs during the day. About two years ago, we found a caregiver for Em whom we trust and fits like an extension of our family; she has made a huge difference as we have continued to shift into better life balance.

I found myself feeling lighter as I drove to work, because I was able to experience some hours where I functioned outside of the strain of Em's pain and worry about her future wellbeing. However, I sometimes had a sense of suspended reality, because my work and home lives felt unconnected and the disconnect made me feel inauthentic. I did not want to compartmentalise my life and, though it was difficult to speak about, I began sharing the details of what had happened openly at work.

That sharing made a big difference for me. As I learned to open up, I received many insights, opinions, and judgments from people with whom I was interacting. I received empathy and valued so much those people who held space for me. I also remember the advice from a co-worker to keep my personal life separate from my work life, because pretending all was well would improve people's perception of me. Processing that piece of advice was critical as it shaped my philosophy before I could move forward at work. Ultimately, I realised I could not give my best to anyone, unless I was presenting myself honestly. Though it is sometimes scary, it has also opened the door to allow healing, self-acceptance, and improved coherence in all the facets of my life.

Medical persons were advocating to "allow Em to go", to put her in a home and proceed with our lives, and even to plan a hysterectomy for her (it shocked and dismayed us that someone would bring this up for us when she was just 10 months old). On a daily basis, we were dealing with a good measure of guilt, fear, and worry. We had some added pressures as one or two family members called us incredulous about Em's brain injury. We found ourselves comforting and helping them accept that Em had been brain injured and bedridden. We also journeyed through sadness and roaring anger as some loved ones levied their opinions that we had caused Emma's injuries. Those experiences really shook me up. For a while, I gave in to the temptation to self-isolate and stop trusting others. Looking back, I recognise that people's judgments and opinions served a purpose: as painful as they were to navigate, they forced us to clarify our own positions and decide how we saw Emma and ourselves. We came to realise that no-one else's judgment mattered as we had to navigate the life we were living.

At the same time, our then six-year-old son was taking care of himself more than we realised. He brought home a report card in which he earned 100% in every single subject, and we were amazed and happy to have that unexpected boon. But not everything that looks shiny turns out to be good. I sadly learned a few years later that he was insisting on perfection from himself because he did not want to burden us more than we already were. He was constantly soothing and hovering over his sister. He was hugging us and speaking to us like a little parent. And I, walking through my life in a daze, recognised nothing off-balance until anger began to leak out of him a few years later.

There were also times I felt like I was witnessing God's miracles and an effervescent joy would fill me. One such time happened when I was doing a music therapy course to try to learn skills that I could parlay into daily support at home for Emma. I had gotten some plastic Easter eggs from the pharmacy and filled them with raw split peas (dhal) to make little shakers. Holding Emma's hand around a shaker, I had made up a little song and watched her squeal in delight at the sound and vibration against her palm. I put the shaker on her highchair tabletop and swiped her hand at it. Her laughter filled my heart. Then silence, as I waited. Another swipe from me to get the rattle sound. Laughter. Silence. Then I said, "Emma's turn." Silence. Waiting. Up came her little hand, just by a few millimetres, but clearly an attempt to engage to get the sound. I shook the shaker and she joyfully laughed. Tears filled my eyes, and I couldn't stop laughing. I kept it together and we took turns again and again, until the exercise ended in kisses and hugs and holding her close as I danced around and sang for her. She squealed in delight at the whirling movements.

How do you feel?

I share snippets of our experiences in the first few years following Emma's injury because they chart the many lows the journey drags one through, but also remind you that there will also be some transcendent and unexpected highs that you will treasure forever.

I encourage you to hide from none of your feelings. You may find you put yourself in a sort of numb middle ground emotionally, because that keeps you from feeling the depth of pain, vitriol or anger set off by what you are experiencing. I believe that such numbing is a coping mechanism to help us survive the extreme pressure we may be under. The numbness may seem like a good thing and, in the short term, I think it is, but I don't think it should become the state in which we live permanently. That's because when you have joyful times, you may find that your numbness doesn't let you truly feel it either. We need to find our way back to experiencing life fully.

Over time, I allowed myself to feel my negative and positive emotions more authentically, and that only happened in slow motion as I came to learn how to really cope with all the brokenness that lived inside me from experiences as far back as my early childhood and coming all the way up to when Emma was hurt and our journey from there.

My friend, I know that taking stock of how you feel is not likely a task that can happen in a single moment when you declare to yourself, "Let me face my feelings". However, I want to encourage you to look within and get your feelings out for your own sake. Writing helps, or recording a voice recording on a phone. What happened? Where did it start going out of control? What is the last joyful moment you remember before things shifted? What marked the shift? What series of events followed? What was said to you? What did you say? What did you receive through your senses? What did you express using those senses? What thoughts did you have as things progressed? What feelings?

You don't have to do this publicly; in fact, it may feel so much better to do this all by yourself. Just give yourself over and let yourself really feel your emotions. Sometimes, having a friend to talk to, or sharing the sense of loss with your spouse can be exactly right.

In my case, the first time I truly faced my pain was about a year after we returned home. Sean had gone to work, and I was taking care of Emma during the day; when he came home, he would assume duty and I would head off to my evening teaching. My back was hurting, and I was hunched over and dragging my right leg. Despite the pain, I had just lifted Em into the bathroom and bathed her and massaged her and dressed her and sung to her. Now I had her propped against my left arm as I fed her some milk.

Suddenly I was crying: big wracking sobs as I told her how sorry I was that all of this had happened to her, how much I loved her and wished I could take away all this hurt and limitation from her. I just kept apologising and crying these big, open-mouthed

Look within and get your feelings out for your own sake.

ACKNOWLEDGING WHAT HAPPENED

sobs in the privacy of my home with the only witness being my blind, wordless child who could not see me cry or tell anyone what had happened. Without warning, Emma began to laugh so loudly and joyfully and the more I cried the more she laughed because, to her, my crying sounded like laughter.

I didn't discern the lesson then, but I have since thought back on it. There I was, labelling my child as "in pain" because I was measuring her against my standard of "normal" and finding her lacking. I was deriving my pain from the lens through which I was seeing our situation. But, even as I cried out of what I thought was empathy for her, did she really have pain? Not in that moment: just then, she had pure (and very loud) joy. I was projecting my pain because I was not yet being honest about what I felt. I needed to feel all those feelings honestly, and though I am writing about it, I know I have not finished my own tour of my emotions related to our journey with Emma.

I don't know what is to come, but thus far, I have felt such a range of lows, including "poor me", despair, frustration, begging God for a miracle, anger, isolation, jealousy as I watched other children cry loudly while my child could not make a sound, and bereftness as I watched a friend's seven-year-old daughter (also named Emma) walk about with her mom while Em remained bedridden at the same age. I have felt judged and belittled by doctors and therapists and family and strangers in clinics and on the street. I have doubted myself and hated myself for my weakness and my fear. I have taken out my frustration on my husband and even my son when the poison of self-blame has built up and erupted. I have cried in hopelessness and fear when Emma has been screaming from the pain due to her challenges.

And I feel shame, too. Once, an aunt and uncle showed up unannounced on my porch. I was still in my nightie at midmorning, bathing Emma and looking bedraggled. I felt so small before their eyes. I have felt abandoned by God and my family and friends more times than I can say. I have felt blamed and resentful, like the time an aunt told me it was my fault Emma was brain-injured because I opted for her to have surgery. I have cried and worried over finances, long-term care needs, a growing list of expensive equipment, risks of keeping Emma safe and also having a son to serve with dwindling funds, energy and time.

I have berated myself for not having it all together to a better degree. When I work on my business, I tell myself I should be doing more therapy with Emma. When I spend time with Emma, I tell myself I should be working on my business to change our financial situation. Sometimes the cycles of guilt are endless. Sometimes, I have felt so bone tired that I have wished it would all end so I can rest and then feel shame again because I am being so selfish.

And what of the highs? There have thankfully been those as well. I have felt the certainty that this life is a massive blessing because I have been able to share this journey with exactly the right family of souls who fit me and love me. I have felt my heart become buoyant with the lightness of Emma's laugh. I have sat holding Emma against my chest at 2 am and seen the glint of her bright eyes in the darkness and felt borne up by her absolute trust and love for me. I have felt motivated to be a better person because I think this challenge is pushing me to become stronger and serve others who are also on this sort of journey with their children. I have been inspired to create therapy materials and routines and songs and beats to serve Emma's needs. I have felt such fulfilment from that burgeoning creativity that I'm learning to ignore the voice inside that tells me to hide my voice and face because they are imperfect, and let those imperfections touch my child and others with love and trust and hope of service and inspiration.

> *This life is a massive blessing...I have felt my heart become buoyant with the lightness of Emma's laugh.*

What should you do?

In line with the title of this chapter, my best advice to you is to allow yourself to really feel what you are living through with your child. Detail your situation as you lived it and felt it. Reflect on it. Lean into your emotions, both the low frequency ones that we label as "bad" and the high frequency ones that modern culture finds more acceptable. There is no shame in being angry, crying, talking to others, writing it out, or otherwise expressing your feelings. Get it out as long and as often as you need. If you have the financial ability, it might be a good idea to lean on a professional for trained support, or to enrol yourself in activities that could let you expel your emotions by getting physically active or creatively expressing yourself. Definitely, if you can, get help with the overwhelm of managing the multiple moving parts of your newly complexified home and work life. A competent caregiver, nurse, or assistant would be a blessing.

You are doing nothing wrong when you take some time for self-care; in fact, you'd be doing something very good not only for your health but also the health of your broader family.

At some point you will realise you aren't stuck in the pain of the past quite as much, and you may feel more ready to assess where you are now. That is something so exciting to me because then you are ready to step back and look at the whole picture. Recognise that no matter how hard the past is (or the future will be), or how much pain we carry and feel because of it, that past is not in our control. The only control we have is in this current moment, so focus on accepting where you are, giving yourself a pat on the back, and recognising that past-you did the best you could have done.

To conclude, settle into knowing that nobody else's judgement of you counts. What matters is what you think and what you feel in your current situation, and so I hope you are rounding up this chapter with a sense of readiness to look within. Face what you can face now and be gentle enough with yourself to admit what you can't face yet.

Your Checklist

✓ Be gentle with yourself about what happened.
  - ☐ Remember that we cannot change the past, but we can change our response to it; we can change how it affects us.

✓ Allow yourself to feel your feelings.
  - ☐ How did you feel then?
  - ☐ How do you feel now?
  - ☐ Both your positive and negative feelings are valid and important.
  - ☐ What are you not ready to open up to feeling yet? Revisit and tune in further over time.

✓ Try various tools and approaches to see how different ones may help you to connect with and process feelings at different times and in different ways.
  - ☐ Shout, cry to express anger, shame, fear, hate, jealousy, worry etc.
  - ☐ Talk with a trusted friend or counsellor.
  - ☐ Keep your insights private but explore them by journaling.
  - ☐ Get physically active.
  - ☐ Connect through your creativity.
  - ☐ Picture yourself as someone else that you are listening/talking to and being gentle toward.

Maybe you'll ask what to do to deal with the worries of the future but, in this moment, just let those worries flow by as if they are on a breeze. We'll cover that in another chapter. For now, take a little time to be gentle and loving toward yourself, because you've been through a lot, and if you were viewing someone else's story you would be a lot gentler and more forgiving to them than you are with yourself.

CHAPTER 2

Coping with the Situation Today

Deal with Today

SO, MY FRIEND, you're immersed in some tough times. If you're feeling anything like what I have felt, you might be wondering how you're going to get through it, and you may not be seeing enough (or any) bright spots just about now in your life. You might be asking yourself: *How can I get through this?* Especially if the situation seems unlikely to change or likely to get even more complicated as time passes.

Getting through today gets easier when we don't weigh ourselves down with yesterday or tomorrow. It is so easy to grieve or lay blame as we look into the past (and there is a time when you may have to just face all those painful thoughts and feelings). It is also natural to start building plans and dreams up in your head or on paper (and there will

> *Getting through today gets easier when we don't weigh ourselves down with yesterday or tomorrow.*

also be a time for that). However, if things are feeling overwhelming, if you have a never-ending to-do list that is shutting you down, my own experience has shown me to press pause on every single thing other than what I must do IN THIS MOMENT.

The One Thing

This approach simplifies your day, your hour, your very minute, and that allows you to just breathe and do one thing at a time. No matter how difficult that one thing may be, it is only one thing. So, do that. And then focus on the next "one thing" and the next, and you will get through the day.

I know life is meant to be more, but this is the gift to give yourself and your family right now. This is the mindful approach that allows you be present and cope with your situation in a sustainable way.

When Emma was in rehab, a doctor had been lazy about seeing to her and caused a chemical burn to the site of her gastrostomy tube. The day after the burn, she was discharged, and I flew home with her to our country. My husband was terrified to touch her because she was in endless pain. We could see her tears, but they fell in silence because she could not make sounds. I was cleaning the wound, dressing it twice a day, and feeding her and cradling her and crying in secret. I was wrestling with my own guilt because I had told the doctor she was doing it wrong but allowed her to give me a dressing down for challenging her. Then, I stood by and watched her hurt my child. Now, we could not find a window for even a few hours of sleep night or day as we saw to her needs while also caring for our then six-year-old son. We were worried about each other and worried about how to

No matter how difficult that one thing may be, it is only one thing.

keep juggling everything including finding medical care and therapy services as well as staying on at work to pay the bills.

I had to just tell myself, "One decision at a time, one action at a time, one project at a time" and that was how I got through the first few years. Looking back, it feels like I sleepwalked through part of it. I shifted my work hours to evenings, and the elements that did not require me to be physically at work I would do every night in one- or two-hour windows as Emma slept. As soon as Sean drove into our driveway at 3pm, I would race into the shower and get out of the house to commute an hour and start teaching my students at 5pm. And over time, I found a way to trust Em to someone else's care for part of the day, in order to see to extensive work demands that I had to meet to keep my job.

You may be asking how to decide on a single thing when it feels like there are multiple demands bombarding you every single second. The fact is that you can only do one thing at a time, so it comes down to prioritisation. In the beginning, it is likely that you will prioritise the most urgent thing, the crying child, the food cooking on the stove, the pinging alarm. It is human nature to give attention to the squeaky wheel.

However, if we always default to the urgent tasks, many of them will not be the most important ones that deserve your attention and some of the important things will go unaddressed, potentially forever. These are things like your own self-care, better support for your other children and your relationship, your long-term health and fitness, financial matters, and the like. The first one is important enough that we are touching on it next. All the rest will be addressed later in the book.

Self-care

I want you to remember that if you run yourself into the ground, you will not be there for anyone, not yourself, not your work, not your family, not your child who depends so absolutely on you. So, part of tackling "the one thing" must be finding a few minutes for caring for yourself. I'll be honest, I know this to logically be true, but my heart tends to put the rest of my priorities ahead of my own care. Until I break down. Get sick. Start worrying intensely. Lose the energy to drag myself to the next thing. Start getting angry at being asked to take something else on. All of that can be avoided if we just carve out a little sliver of our time for our own well-being.

Back when Emma was newly hurt, I felt there was no time for self-care, and I certainly had no one advocating for me. But you're reading this, and I'm thrilled to be able to advocate for you. Here's my advice on setting aside time for self-care.

Start fresh

One thing I remember was that, in the beginning, I would be woken up by my crying child, and I would move straight into firefighting mode. Many days, it would be 1 p.m. before I realised I was still in my nightie and had not brushed my teeth yet. Most days, I would not have eaten until 11 a.m. either. Your first step is to give yourself the minimum level of care: start your day with a shower, time to brush your teeth, and having breakfast. If you think breakfast takes time you don't have, grab a banana or have a pre-made smoothie in the fridge. That certainly helps me feel more primed to face whatever challenges I face now. Added advantage: if someone shows up at your door unannounced, you won't feel mortified to be seen as a dirty mess.

Relieve stress

The second step is to make time to just relieve stress for a few minutes during the day. We have found ways to incorporate this into our work and play time with Emma. For example, Emma's favourite person in the whole world is Sean and (other than his children) his favourite thing in the whole world is listening to the news—so he lies next to her and reads the news aloud to her. Win-win! The news may be my least favourite thing, so my own self-care includes never being around when he does that!

Another way we have been able to just steal a moment for stress relief throughout the day is taking a few minutes to ground ourselves. To ground myself, I just sit and imagine my stresses flowing into the ground like poison draining out of me and being absorbed into the earth. I picture the earth cleaning my negative energy the way it cleans dirty water and then sends us clean water. I complete the grounding exercise by picturing the warmth and healing of the earth and of nature, radiating up my legs and filling me with cleansing power and strength.

As for breathing, I mentioned earlier in the book that I do a deep breathing variation where I breathe in for four counts, hold for four counts and breathe out for four counts. Deep, slow breathing goes a long way to calm nerves and slow your heart rate, while shallow, fast breathing will amp up your adrenalin and excitement and heart rate. My heart health has improved since I started the grounding and deep breathing practices.

You can find many other lovely breathing and grounding exercises if you do a google search.

Cause Your Child Less Stress

I also advise you to cause your child less stress when doing the activities that you must do with them. There are some things that are critical and must be done if recovery is to be supported, even if pain is involved, and in those cases I acknowledge that we have to grit our teeth and bear it. However, there will be ways you can vary activities to make many of them more enjoyable and even turn them into play.

I'll share our experience to illustrate. In the beginning, Emma could neither see, hear, nor make sounds, and even light touch was painful to her. All of this made daily therapy very stressful for her, and it was heart-breaking to know we were causing her pain even as we tried to help her. Needless to say, our own stress levels skyrocketed whenever therapy was in progress. I became an active observer whenever therapy was being done. I observed the therapist's attitude, her choice of words, whether her body language communicated hope or fatalistic despair as to Emma's chances. And what became clear was that Emma's response correlated with the therapist's attitude. Therapists could say the right thing, but I could see which of them looked lovingly and positively at her and which ones squirmed or were hopeless about her sad condition. For the former, Emma would valiantly battle to do what they asked of her. With the latter, she would scream until she threw up.

That was invaluable life experience for us; we learned to shift to happiness and excitement when we were doing home therapy sessions. We also started using an integrative approach. It was no longer about attending a therapy hour that Emma would be forced to endure. We found therapists who interacted with Emma in ways that she perceived as joy-inducing. In the time when she could not hear, we noticed that she seemed to pick up the vibrations from music and so music was always being played. We tried different forms of touch and just counterbalanced those that caused pain with positive reinforcers like kisses until she began to love touch again. Then slowly, we pushed the boundaries to where slight new aspects of touch became acceptable to her. Now, she has a full body massage after a bath twice a day, and it is one of the things she laughs loudest for.

And finally, I was thrilled that Emma's ability to hear returned over time, and so music has emerged as our number one therapy tool. We use sound to soothe and to excite her, to get her moving to maintain muscle tone, and to calm her down at night-time. And the best music appears to be our voices singing to her. As Emma began to come alive to us singing and talking with her, we started reading to her and doing action songs like The Wheels on the Bus. While the music filled her with joy, it allowed us to sneak in more physical activity, maintaining her muscle tone and increasing her range of motion. Certainly, that has taken stress away from us as well. Interventions do not have to drain your child or feel like work to have positive impacts on your child physically, mentally, or emotionally.

In summary, my advice on causing your child less stress is to get to know which senses open the door to the most joy for them and let those be the way to connect with and show love to your child, as well as to become creative in building your therapy approaches around those senses at home. If you want some tips on how to play around with merging senses with therapy ideas, I'll share some adaptations in the therapy chapter of this book.

Put Things in Place for the Future

There is an Aesop's Fable "The Ant and the Grasshopper" in which the point is made that we cannot only live for today because we must also plan for the future. This is always important, but perhaps never more so than when we have long-term care of a loved one to think about. There is a whole chapter dedicated to financial planning for the future support of your special needs child, but in the next few paragraphs, let's talk about shorter term future-planning.

I assume your immediate needs include getting income to meet your day-to-day living needs, and with a special needs child, I'd understand if you are wondering how you can pull off being a full-time caregiver and a full-time income-earner.

The first temptation for me was to just stop working immediately and become Emma's full-time carer. Especially for a mom, this may be the gut instinct. More intrusively, external expectations about your role may put added pressure on you, and the judgment from others, even those who love you, is hurtful. Know that this decision is in the sole power of yourself and other parent(s)/guardians of your child. It does take a lot of personal power to push aside outside opinions and follow your own heart. At least, it did for me.

My advice is to not just blindly follow your heart, because this decision also needs have some input from your head. You need to be able to afford living expenses as you did before you had your special needs child, and now you also need to be able to manage costs of routine medical visits, emergencies that may come up, therapy, medicine, special dietary needs, special equipment, home adaptations, and more. Whether or not you hold a job, you will likely find the need to also afford caregiving support. For some, the support may be for short periods when you must leave your child home, or you may need someone with you at home to help with lifting, therapy, other aspects of care, or home management. So, while the idea that love will triumph over all may be powerful, please carefully consider the consequences of giving up your job.

If you decide to hold on to a job, there are options available. Will you keep the exact same job with the exact same hours, will you seek more flexible hours in your full-time job, will you shift to a part-time job or will you find a way to work from home so that you stay close to your child?

No matter which of the above options you are drawn to, you need to have at least one person (and ideally several more people) that you can trust and depend upon. You'd be able to lean on them to free you up when you are at your wits end and need some time to yourself, if you are sick and need to go to the doctor, if you are longing for a few hours "off" to just manage overwhelm, and a host of other reasons.

I'm sure you already know how scary it is to trust someone else to look after your child. Please remember that if you don't already have someone who can do this and you have an emergency, your child will likely end up in the care of a person with whom your child is unaccustomed. This will stress both you and your child much more than if you start putting things in place to vet a few people, let them get comfortable with providing care while you support them to deliver the standard of care that you expect.

If you are in the position of a single parent without extended family support, having a support person is most critical of all. I look at the single parents in Emma's clinic and feel such respect for the powerhouses that they are. But no man is an island, and I pray you find the supportive and loving person who can step in as a suitable caregiver to supplement your efforts. You will definitely need to make a list of attributes you consider necessary in such a caregiver. For me the list kept morphing and the latest version includes nursing training (because of Em's severe medical needs and risks coupled with her rapid growth in recent years, we needed someone who could do CPR and had been trained in proper lifting techniques), Em's comfort with them to the point where she would eat from them and relax around them, sensitivity and compassion about her challenges and medical history, and a feeling that the caregiver is an extension of our family unit.

If you are co-parenting with a spouse, significant other, or ex, you need to have a planning session to look at how to schedule responsibilities and trade off time. I tend to fulfil more of the duties related to therapy visits and singing and at home play-therapy integration work. Sean handled most of the feeding and bathing tasks after Em's feeding tube was removed. It is important to say that Emma's nurse has been a lifesaver in supplementing our care with therapy, feeding, and bathing. Sean also spends nights with Emma, because I am unable to lift her now that she is physically taller and heavier.

I'll be honest; there is so much more that we need to do better in terms of our trade-offs. I recently lifted Em and dislocated my collarbone; my intention this year is to work on building my strength so I can lift Em more capably and not depend entirely on Sean. Sean needs more sleep, so we have started scheduling a couple of hours of sleep time for him during the day. And when we get into dreaming really big, we even imagine that one day, we'll be able to spend a little time together. That deserves to be scheduled because our marriage is what is keeping this family afloat, and we need to stay attuned to who our spouse is and how our spouse thinks, outside of the special needs topics and our task list.

Conclusion

I hope you are feeling the desire to delve into how you want to approach your now-management, from mixing mindfulness and self-care, to planning how to step into the short-term future, especially with regard to providing for your family and leaving some space to give yourself support. It is so important to be compassionate to your special needs child, but you also deserve to be compassionate to yourself. I want you to thrive even as you walk through this part of your journey.

Your Checklist

In case you haven't taken notes, here's a little checklist of the big takeaways from this chapter.

✓ Be present.
- ☐ Let go of the pain of the past.
- ☐ Let go of the worry about the future.
- ☐ Stay focused on "one thing" at a time.
- ☐ Learn to prioritise important things, not only urgent things.

✓ Schedule precious time for self-care each day.
- ☐ Shower and brush your teeth and have breakfast.
- ☐ Incorporate your favourite activities into the routine duties with your child.
- ☐ Practice deep breathing and grounding.
- ☐ Have someone you can lean on to provide care for your child other than you and any other guardians.

✓ Turn therapy into fun for your child.
- ☐ Have a positive attitude because your child feels that.
- ☐ Observe what activities give your child joy and adapt therapy accordingly.

CHAPTER 3

Managing Aloneness and Isolation

YOU ARE SUCH a powerhouse in my mind, and I hope you feel the truth of that. I know that you are powering through challenges just by continuing to get up every day and face the demands that are a part of your life. My eyes are teary imagining some of the things you may be facing, but I also have a huge grin on my face. That is exactly how it is, right? We get such awful lows as well as such transcendent highs because of this journey we're on as special needs parents and, as my friend Lauren pointed out to me, maybe that means that we get to experience a wider range of emotions than many others in the course of our lives.

In this chapter, I want to explore one particular challenge that took me close to my breaking point and forced me to choose whether or not I would allow myself to spiral ever lower into negativity. Though I don't know for sure, my gut tells me every special needs parent experiences it: isolation.

If you have felt isolation, was it a silence and aloneness related to feeling as if you were unseen and unimportant? Was it a retreat of most (if not all) of your family and friends that made you feel as though you were a leper who was being scorned and given a wide berth? Was it that although you were surrounded by people, nobody could relate, thereby leaving you feeling lonely? Maybe your experience with isolation is different, but I want to explore a few of the ways isolation might show up for us and offer some approaches that could bolster you.

Facets of Isolation

When your child is born with special needs or becomes hurt so that they develop special needs, the change in your life is sudden. Being alone (just you or just your family) to face this huge life challenge can really crush you emotionally and mentally. Isolation descends without warning. For me, it was one of the hardest things to cope with, and I remember longing to talk about it but not being able to because sometimes people couldn't understand. Sometimes they told me to stop complaining and suck it up. Mostly, I didn't feel like I could unload such heavy life issues on an unsuspecting person.

Nobody prepares us for what is to come. Even if there was some kind of course to prepare us, I don't think there could be anything that eases us into the emotional wasteland that follows. This lack of understanding and preparedness makes the isolation creep up unexpectedly. It is shocking when we look back and realise the depth of loneliness and despair under which we have become buried.

Isolation ramps up the older our child gets, in most cases. As our child gets older, larger, sicker, needier, the demands on us increase and, for those of us whose children cannot move themselves well or at all, our child's mobility decreases so we become more isolated as we find it harder to get outside with our child. Typically, our only regular contact outside of our immediate household would be caregivers, doctors, and therapists. It takes a very special extended family member, friend, neighbour, or church-mate to keep coming back to visit us; if you have this person, know they are golden!

Feelings of abandonment

Many times, you will feel abandoned and unloved by those who were closest to you. I recall telling a friend what happened following Em's brain injury, and she very quickly said, "Oh, everything will be alright," and ended the call. The next time I heard from her was six years later, when she called to ask for a phone number to arrange lessons for her son.

People you once thought would be at your side in your darkest hours will disappear, many in a split second. We experienced that with neighbours, friends, even close family members. It was so widespread that I felt I had been shut out like people were quarantining for fear they contract our disease. With very few exceptions, there were no visits, and no phone calls when we returned with our child in her brain injured, bedridden state.

I could not make sense of this for years. I could not understand how people whom I believed shared my values, whom I believed were good and caring people could suddenly become distant, uncaring people. How, suddenly, could they stop loving me and my family and cast us out? To the extent that I can, I have constructed a framework of understanding to help me to cope.

I believe that when most people look at us, they see the pain of our situation, the horror of what happened to Em, the hopelessness of her prognosis, and not necessarily us as people. They see us only in comparison to "normal" and maybe that sparks fear, or guilt, or pity. Maybe it sparks a level of discomfort because they would prefer to live without having to see the messiness and imperfection of our life. Instead of facing that fallibility, they curate a prettier environment for themselves by removing what they perceive as *unpleasant*.

> I felt cast-out and that spiralled me into feeling I was not worthy, not good enough as a person.

What feelings does that abandonment spark when you feel it? For me, I felt resentment, anger, a bone-deep sadness, and even shame that so many of my closest people could not find enough love for me to support me when I needed them most. I felt cast-out and that spiralled me into feeling I was not worthy, not good enough as a person.

The invisibility of your isolation

Something that surprised, angered and hurt me for a long time was accepting that people can't even recognise your situation when it is playing out right in front of them. The following example, experienced with my closest family, is not intended to hurt them. Instead, it is to show how easy it is for isolation to descend upon you, even when you've been included in an invitation to meet up.

Sean had spent a sleepless night, so I'd insisted on taking Em with me and Bry to a family luncheon so he could sleep for some quiet hours while we were gone. Bry, his cousins, and everyone else gathered around the table for lunch. I sat in the TV room, where I had Emma propped on some high pillows, and I fed her there. I could hear the sounds of everyone laughing and chatting, and every now and again, they would call out to me to say come join them. It was an exercise in isolation, since nobody who had finished eating thought to offer to stay with Em so I could go eat and have a little chat too. When Bry thought to check on me, he brought some food so I could eat where I was sitting next to Em on the sofa.

Was it that the other adults were being insensitive? I don't think they intended to hurt me or exclude me. I just think people expected I would be with my child and my aloneness became invisible. We seem to be the only ones who understand the loneliness in which we are mired. It feels like we will always be on the outside looking in.

Sure, I have Em's sweet laugh and innocence with me, but some adult company and conversation would also be nice in a social setting. Even better if both my husband and I can interact together in that setting, but it bears mentioning that even when we are together somewhere, one of us stays with Em while the other eats or talks with people. We are forever trading places.

It is interesting how going out can exacerbate the feeling of isolation by setting our circumstances in counterpoint to the relative freedom of others. Our level of stress also rises because we are placed in unfamiliar settings with fewer resources to care for our child. Add to it that people generally watch us askew as our child, and the efforts we make to care for our child, stand out from most others, leading to people having behind-hand and sometimes audible conversations about what they observe, prognose, and predict. It becomes pretty unsettling and stressful sometimes, and it takes some effort to psych yourself up to go somewhere, knowing you will open yourself up to yet another isolating experience.

Being stuck at home

It is very demanding to move around with our special needs children. When Em was younger, she was highly stressed by noise, new places, or people she did not know. She would cry, scream, vomit. We couldn't go around with her much, even though physically she was an infant. As she got older, she became more tolerant of noise and open to being around people a little more. However, she is physically very tall and heavy and unable to move herself. It has become a real struggle just to move her from the bed to the rocking chair two feet away from the bed.

So why don't we suck it up and power through and take Em around? To go anywhere with Em requires so much effort and physical work, plus we need her stroller and a host of materials in case she has an accident and must be changed, food, water, everything you'd carry with you for a baby but sized up for the body and care of a nine-year-old. Plus, when we get to the hospital, the park, the wherever, and Em needs to be changed, what facilities are there to change a nine-year-old with the needs of a baby? When she cries or flails, how easy is it to manage her large body while she is sitting on my lap or unrelentingly pressing her own legs against the tabletop above her legs? How easy is it to cope with once again being the hub of all the stares from strangers who are experiencing a range of emotions from curiosity to empathy to irritation to judgement of my parenting flaws? We feel safer, less physically and mentally strained and less at-risk in our home, and likely you feel that way too. Yet being alone in our home, the isolation sits heavy on our heart, and facing these realities ramps up the grief and anxiety and stress and sadness.

Feeling left behind

Just watching the world move on exacerbates isolation. We see the people we were once so connected with moving forward with their families, with their children going to new school years, on vacations, doing extra-curricular activities. We remain tied to the same medical and therapy routines in institutions and in our homes. I smile as I see other parents thriving, but it also hurts and sometimes I have cried, because their journeys are moving them away from us. We are left behind and even more alone, cognisant that they have nothing in common with us and are moving on. Watching others move into another level at school, while my child can't go to school even one day. Watching someone dance in a concert when Em can't hold a spoon or hold up her head can underscore the feeling that we keep marking time as the world marches on.

Blame

Another cause of isolation is blame. I've met so many people who want to assign blame, and so often they feel the need to let me know that the blame rests with me. Emma had an ICU nurse who decided that Sean and I resembled each other and actually asked me if I had married my cousin! That would certainly have allowed her to decree that I had caused my child's heart problems. There was also the aunt who felt compelled, while sitting in my porch, to tell me that it was my fault that Emma had been brain damaged, since I was the one who had taken Emma for open heart surgery. There is nothing like those little doses of judgment to push you out of the warm embrace of belonging and "otherise" you.

Financial concerns

The state of finances can also exacerbate isolation. So many special needs parents find their income being channelled largely to medicine, doctor and therapy visits, surgery and recovery, mobility equipment, caregiver support, and many more things for their special needs child. They find it hard to even manage their other expenses. So even with the very improbable likelihood that they had the time or energy to go on a dinner date or a vacation, how would they be able to afford it? That's yet another limitation that keeps them cloistered at home and unable to move about the way friends and family are able to.

Mask-wearing

We are trained in modern society to present ourselves as though we have it all well in hand, sorted, under control. And to present that, we tend to put up a front. I call that mask-wearing. The cool demeanour we assume to look like we can handle the vomiting child in the middle of the therapy session while everybody stares at you and whispers behind their hands. The straight back when the doctor says you're being irresponsible to think your child can ever improve, or you hear you should really get more therapy sessions or surgery booked, but you know the cost will break the bank. The fake smile you give when you meet someone and hold back the truth about your child's condition because you know they didn't really want to hear the uncomfortable truth when they said, "Hi, how are you?"

Why are you wearing masks? Maybe to convey yourself as having it all together, being brave, being confident, being happy, being the devoted parent, being gentle, being unflappable? And there is another set of reasons we wear those masks. We hide our pain and fear and push down our truth because we don't want other people to think we might be complaining, or uncaring of our child, or jealous of their freedom, or sad to have lost so much of the agency we once had in our lives.

Tackle Isolation

We first need to be honest with ourselves about what we are experiencing, what we are feeling, and why we might be feeling it. Only when we do that, are we going to be able to set out what our hopes are for ourselves and our families and begin crafting and executing strategies and actions to usher in change. This is true for our isolation as with so much else in our lives. Here are some of the simple approaches that have made, and continue to make, a difference for me.

Connect with yourself

Come to terms with your feelings. Knowing exactly what you feel is half of the battle and needs to happen before you can take any corrective action to try to heal. Journaling and meditation have been extremely useful for me in this regard. When I can't talk to anyone else, I can talk it out with myself through my written words. I can express it in poetry and through my art.

Build connection at home

You might start by enhancing your relationship with those in your home: your spouse, your children. Even simple things build this connection. For example, we recently put a hammock into Emma's room as rocking will soothe her. It has caused Bryan to spend more time there as he loves using the hammock. He lies with Emma beside him sometimes, and sometimes he watches his online classes as he swings. We have more relaxed conversations with him, and we have been laughing more together.

Make an effort to visit (in person) with others beyond your nuclear family. If leaving your home is almost impossible, then you can reach out and invite one or two friends to your home. I do recognise how difficult this can be, both emotionally/psychologically as well as physically, in terms of balancing the demands of your child while people are visiting you. This has not happened much with us, but just this week, my sister visited, and I invited her to come to Em's room while I fed her. She dry-brushed Em's limbs and sang to Em as I fed Em. It was such a healing time for me. I genuinely felt more connected with my sister in that 30-minute visit than any other time we have been together in several years. Opening up might feel uncomfortable and risky but you must push yourself into new modalities if you want to eventually discover which version works best for you and your child.

Connect with other special needs parents

The one group of people who will get you best would be other special needs parents, so find ways to build a community with them. This community will see and hear you, and you will also be able to give empathy and compassion even as you receive them. In this group, you may find it easier to drop your masks and talk openly without worrying whether people will think you are selfish or incompetent or lazy.

Count your blessings

Our lives with our special needs children come with many blessings as well as challenges. It is absolutely important to take stock of the blessings that came into our lives with our special needs child. Reminding ourselves of the amazing joy our child has brought into our life really ramps up our gratitude and pushes back the isolation. One way in which I have done this is writing poems and letters to Emma. Celebrating the light she has shone and continues to shine into my life, the growing she has sparked, and the love she has inspired me to give, receive, and observe.

Connect with God

When I have been most broken, the thing that has come naturally to me has been to pray. Prayer has helped me cry about troubles, worries, pains, and loneliness to God, and I have genuinely felt held and supported in those moments. Prayer has helped me to persevere another day and, more and more, I have noticed that my prayers are increasingly shifting from fear and pain to gratitude and belief in Emma's healing.

Share your story

Sharing your story is so important! Your story will build connection with others, give you a boost, help you support and encourage others, and even open you up to learning about approaches others have used that could help your child. Can you imagine how much light this could bring into special needs circles and also into your own household?

Connect with online communities

Connection with others is a major way to dial down your isolation. One of the most transformative strategies for me was connecting with people online. My connections began to be forged a few years after Em was hurt. They happened when I began doing short online training programs. I would share with other participants about lessons learned in the courses, and as we chatted back and forth, friendships sometimes blossomed. Years later, many of those friendships have persevered and those connections have made me feel loved, appreciated, and encouraged. Without knowing it, those men and women (through their jokes, opinions, and discussions shared with me) shifted me from feeling like an outcast to feel embraced and valued.

> *Finding heart-centred connection is the sword that will defeat the isolation dragon.*

I should note that not all of my communities were related to special needs; what mattered was that the communities consisted of people who were interested in topics of interest to me, and we were able to build accountability and support relationships with one another related to the learning we were doing. Eventually, some relationships deepened to friendship and in some cases, we even got to know each other's families. It is important to share that my husband and son have built connections with a few of my online friends as well. Just last week, Bryan asked about "Aunty Joy" because he had not seen me having a Zoom chat with her in a while.

I am certain that the ultimate cure for isolation is connection: with yourself and with a community that shares your values. Finding heart-centred connection is the sword that will defeat the isolation dragon.

Your Checklist

This chapter explored some of the experiences you may have had with isolation and offered suggestions to help.

✓ Two kinds of isolation are mentioned.
  ☐ Sudden descent into feeling isolated.
  ☐ A slowly worsening sense of isolation.

✓ Feelings of abandonment are explored.
  ☐ Loved ones "disappear" from your life, no calls or visits.
  ☐ People may choose to stay away because your circumstances are uncomfortable for them to face.
  ☐ Not feeling heard.
  ☐ Not feeling cared about.
  ☐ Abandonment can lead you to feel resentment, anger sadness, shame.
  ☐ You may feel cast out, like you are not worthy or not good enough.

✓ What you are experiencing may not be obvious to others.
  ☐ People may take it for granted that you are always with your special needs child.
  ☐ People may not think about helping you or giving you a break.
  ☐ You may feel as though you are on the outside looking in.

MANAGING ALONENESS AND ISOLATION

✓ Isolation can be hard to emerge from due to:
- ☐ A growing child who is hard to physically move around.
- ☐ Lack of facilities to support care of a large special needs child when out in public.
- ☐ Social or other challenges of your child that may limit the scope for exposure to others.
- ☐ Stigmas or judgments handed out to you, including blame being ascribed to you for your child's special needs or condition.
- ☐ The feeling of being scrutinised when you go out with your child, so you are constantly stressed, and it becomes "safer" to just stay in your safe space.
- ☐ Limited finances to afford a caregiver so you can get free time to mingle with others or spend time alone with your significant other.
- ☐ Limited time to connect with others, whether a significant other or social group.
- ☐ Lack of sleep, so that any "free" time should be spent getting a little sleep.
- ☐ Feeling you and your child are being left behind as children their age advance socially and at school and you remain in many of the same medical and therapy and education routines.
- ☐ Finances may be dedicated to managing the necessities for your child and broader family, with little or no extras for vacationing or socialising.
- ☐ The feeling that we must always pretend to have it all under control, instead of asking for help.

✓ Some ways to deal with isolation.
- ☐ Honour yourself and what you are truly feeling.
- ☐ Build connection with those in our home.
- ☐ Invite one or two close friends to your home if you cannot go out easily yourself.
- ☐ Connect with other special needs parents.
- ☐ Connect with people online, especially if you can't build community in person.
- ☐ Don't forget to take stock of your blessings with your special needs child.
- ☐ Lean on God.
- ☐ Share your story; it helps you and others too.

CHAPTER 4

Clarifying Your Powerful Vision

IT IS EASY to lose touch with yourself as you care for a family including a special needs child. Chances are, you'll be prioritising your special child's immediate needs, followed by the needs of the others in your family, followed by the demands of your job, followed by other things on your plate (like your religious group, your community, your extended family, your friends, and so on). Does that sound about right? Look at that list again, now. Do you notice how in the whole run-on list, there was no mention of you? Where do you fit yourself into that list? Where *should* you?

In this chapter, I want to take a pause to just focus on you, to establish what matters most to you, what your intentions and hopes are, to clarify where you are headed, and to give you a little extra oomph by lining up your thoughts, your emotions, and your actions. If you're thinking this sounds like a waste of your time or that you can't afford the time to spend on this chapter, that just may mean that this

> *I want to take a pause to just focus on you.*

chapter has even more value to pass on to you. *I can't say enough how much I think this chapter matters to bolster you as a special needs parent: please focus on it.*

When I was a child, I used to watch an educational children's television show called *Sesame Street*. Maybe you know it. There was a segment with an elephant that walked up to a man who was sitting on a park bench and asked for directions to get to the zoo. The man helpfully began replying, "Go…," to which the elephant—not bothering to listen to the whole response—happily said "thanks" and headed off in the direction of the man's pointed finger. Needless to say, the elephant figured out his slip soon enough and returned to ask for further directions. As the nonsensical truncation of the directions repeated in this humorous piece, the message became clear: if you want to get to your ultimate destination, you not only need to declare where you are headed, but you need to take enough time to get clear on the path to get there.

That is also my message; I encourage you to ensure life doesn't just happen *to* you. Even with the challenges you are facing, you have agency to influence and choose where your life goes more than you might realise. The first step to taking back some of your power is to look within yourself, drawing out what is important to you and what you want in your life.

I had just accepted my dream job of teaching at a University when my daughter was born with unexpected heart issues. Within the first year of getting that job, she went on to need open heart surgery and later to be brain-injured due to a medical mistake. I was living in fear and sorrow most of the time. I certainly did not have a spare second to think about expansion for several of the initial years, because we were fighting so hard to keep our daughter alive, to keep our then five-year-old son feeling he was loved too, and to prop up our stressed marriage. A big worry for me was that I needed to somehow keep delivering at work so I could not only get my lecturing contract extended, but also convert it into a permanent position.

Reflecting back, I can see that I was setting expansion goals; I did have a vision. I was daring to envision that my family would survive the onslaught not only intact but also in love with each other. That I would not only show up at work but also excel at it, and not only be in a contract but also step into job security so there would be less financial risk in our very risk-swamped lives. I did not fulfil all of the vision, at least not in the first five years, but I learned to be resilient, to keep believing and working.

> My family would survive the onslaught not only intact but also in love with each other.

And what is it that led me? When my logic failed me and I could not plan with my brain because of all the overwhelm life had delivered to me, I fell back on the only thing that remained: my intuition. Chances are, you also have intuition guiding you. For me, intuition is the little voice that speaks to me from somewhere around my heart or the centre of my chest. I've heard some people say that it is God speaking to them. I definitely felt like that little, loving, clear voice was a port of endless calm and I always knew what to do, even when we were walking through the years of raging storms. From the flatlining of our daughter, to pain that would cause her to scream and scream until she vomited, to the double dislocation of her hips, that calm voice has kept me sane. It has helped me to focus and keep putting one foot in front of the other during the past eight years.

I wonder, are instances flowing through your mind of situations where you felt supported or guided by your intuition? Writers and other creatives speak of connecting to intuition when they mention their muse, emergency workers rely on both their training and their intuition when swamped by influxes into an emergency room, teachers' intuition plays an important role in understanding and serving their students empathetically and effectively. As a parent, how does your intuition serve you?

Clarify Vision Elements

The first thing I hope you trust me about is to get quiet and connect with yourself, whether you want to call it intuition, inner self, inner light, Spirit, heart of hearts, or some other term. The best and most immediately effective exercise I have ever found to help me do that when I am distracted is a method taught by an amazing intuition teacher, Sonia Choquette, in an exercise she calls "going down the slide".

In this exercise, you breathe deeply in and then fully out (quickly and explosively) three times. Then, on the fourth breath in, before breathing out, open your mouth fully until your open jaws make a clicking sound in your ears; now, with yourself feeling more open of brain and heart, breathe out with an audible yawning sigh as though you are sliding down a slide, long, and peaceful, and releasing.

I always feel extremely relaxed and free as I complete this exercise. I become very heart-connected at the end of that exercise, and it allows me to just be open and tune in to my needs and what to do next.

Now you are ready to spend a little time with yourself. Ask yourself what your hopes and dreams are for the future, specifically. What would you like to have materially, what do you want to be experiencing and doing, and who would you like to be (on the inside) in five years' time? This does not have to be a rewrite of yourself if that is not desired; it could simply be reflective of growth. Jot down a sentence or two about what you want the future to look like in as many of the following areas as you can:

1. Relationship with yourself (knowing and improving your inner self, your values, your character)

2. Relationship with your significant other
3. Relationship with your children
4. Relationship with your extended family and friends
5. Career
6. Spirituality
7. Physical Wellbeing
8. Emotional Wellbeing
9. Financial Wellbeing
10. Intellectual Development
11. Big picture vision (pulling all the others together)

You will undoubtedly find that some of what you envision in one area will overlap with what you write in one or more other areas. That is fine. You don't need stand-alone silos because all of these are bits of the overall vision of a single person: YOU!

Now, although those sentences you have written might be logical or simple statements, they may be making you feel vulnerable. That's because in some of the ideas, you may be connecting your heart to what you say you want to create in your life. That leads us right to the next step in effective visioning: it is time to let yourself connect emotionally to every part of the vision you have begun to set out above.

Emotionally Connect to the Vision

When my intuition began leading me to envision a better future, I really fought against it. I did not want to feel too much pleasure—even in my imagination—because if I allowed myself to feel higher emotional highs, I would also open myself up to feeling lower emotional lows. I didn't believe I could afford to risk that, because my daily life was full of experiences revolving around physical, emotional, mental and financial pain, fear, doubt and loss. To put it plainly, all the challenges of living with a special needs child were threatening to break me, so for several years, I put a wall around my heart and protected myself by living a life where I didn't allow myself to feel things fully. What I did not realise then was that by living that way, I was keeping myself stuck in limbo. Over many years, I allowed myself to risk dreaming and opened myself up more to feeling.

That's what I am hoping you will agree to do, too. I remember how scared I was to dare to feel more, and dream that my life could stretch and become more even with my daughter's situation being the same. I'm thinking maybe you feel the same fear of leaving your safe space and venturing into thinking and dreaming differently. Picture me just two steps ahead of you, stretching my hand back to hold yours as you dare to venture into this new territory.

It is time to connect deeply to the vision elements you wrote above, to tune in with all your senses to the future you want. I first used this approach to write down my itemised vision at age 21 in response to the urging of my father. I lost the paper, and when it turned up again, I was 27. I was shocked to find I had achieved every part of the vision in the five years after I had written it. In the years since, I've encouraged several co-workers and students to put the approach to use too. The version I am passing to you has been enhanced by adding elements from the teachings of Jeffrey Allen, Jon and Missy Butcher, Voldis Forde, and Vishen Lakhiani, to name a few. I have also tweaked the approach myself over the years by plugging in all my senses to really help myself to feel and believe my vision.

STEP 1. Close your eyes and *see yourself* waking up five years into the future. I do not visualise particularly well, so my description of the future state becomes more real to me when I connect all my senses to my vision and either speak it out (recording it) or write it down.

CLARIFYING YOUR POWERFUL VISION

STEP 2. Describe what you hear, see, feel (emotionally and physically), taste, and even smell. Observe who you have become and all that you are surrounded by.

STEP 3. Continue the exercise, moving from a single point in time to allowing yourself to walk through an entire day. Be very specific and give many details as you experience that day.

In the Appendix, I have given you a sample from the most recent version of my vision written in 2020. My vision gets rewritten every year, always taking the previous year's vision as my starting point and letting my intuition guide me to adapt it. When you write your vision, it can feel like fantasy-writing, but you will find that your reality will start to shift in little ways in just a matter of months or weeks. With the clear vision in your mind, and your commitment to it, your actions will become more focused, and the thrill of hope will pulse in your veins. Let me assure you that you are not greedy or fake if you dream big, because I am certain that your vision is one of improving your life AND the lives of many others. Open your heart, *feel* your vision as though it already is your life, trust you deserve it, trust you can give a better life to your special child and your entire family.

Here are some specifics about how to deepen your emotional connection to the vision. My advice is to experience your vision with every single one of your senses. If you are speaking of a garden, are you sitting or standing or walking there? What do you see: what sort of plants? What colours? What heights are they? What insects or other animals are there? Are they moving and making the leaves rustle? Is there a breeze? Can you smell the scent of flowers on the breeze? Is the breeze bringing the sound of a bird with it? Are there benches, hedges, walls, pavers, stepping stones, water features? As you see, hear, touch these things, what do you feel emotionally? Are you experiencing these things with someone else? What is the experience like, having that person with you? Is your child's little hand trustingly in yours as you walk together? How soft is her hand? How do you feel as she turns her face up to yours and you hear her innocent voice making a sweet comment? When I say jump into the envisioned experience, I mean really jump in and feel it, because what you feel impacts you deeply and motivates you massively.

It bears repeating that, just in case you can't actually see the vision, you shouldn't throw out the exercise. Meditation works wonderfully for me. Painting my scenes with words, whether written or audio-recorded, always works beautifully. But you don't even need to do that. You can create a board with electronic or printed images of what you want in your life. As an option you can create a vision board that you can put on your wall (a posterboard or corkboard collage, for example) or as wallpaper for your devices. Pinterest, PowerPoint, and Canva are useful software/online tools for creating electronic versions. I've created a Facebook group called "Lighting the Path" to give my readers a supportive community. You can work on your vision board with other people there.

Fuel Action

By now, I hope you have experienced the kind of visceral charge that you get when you connect your emotions to your logic. A vision is most powerful when the logic of it has been juiced up by plugging in the emotions too. It is this emotion-enhanced vision that will defy all the calls by your brain to give up, to feel tired, to remind you of how long you have been living your mediocre and over-stressed life, to listen to all the naysayers who say you can't, and life is too hard. You will keep demanding change against all odds and working to build the vision specifically because you have already experienced it as though it were real in your visioning exercise.

Conclusion

You have dared to do some dreaming in this chapter. It goes without saying that you must then bridge the gap between where/who you are now and where you will go/who you will become. You don't have all the answers yet, but instead of beating yourself down and saying, "See, you don't have what it takes," you need to play some mind games and say instead, "Just watch me build my competencies and create my best life yet!"

Your Checklist

As a sum up, here are your steps to clarifying and capturing your vision.

✓ Open up to your intuition.
- ☐ If it feels too out there to "tap into your intuition", then just let yourself dream or imagine what you want to create.
- ☐ Press pause on negative emotions so they don't dull your hope and excitement.
- ☐ Use exercises like meditation and/or "going down the slide" to link more strongly to your intuition.

✓ Get clear on your vision.
- ☐ See it in your mind's eye. If seeing is difficult for you, use your words to paint the picture.
- ☐ Build your vision around several elements that come together into a big picture.
- ☐ Connect to it by experiencing your future state and situation with all five physical senses, sight, hearing, smell, taste, and touch.
- ☐ Connect even more deeply by emotionally experiencing the vision.

CLARIFYING YOUR POWERFUL VISION

✓ Capture your vision so you can review it again and again.
- ☐ Write it down using descriptive language to paint the vision with your words.
- ☐ Make an audio recording.
- ☐ Make a vision board by cutting out images and quotes and making a physical collage on posterboard or a cork board.
- ☐ Make an electronic vision board by compiling images online in apps such as Pinterest, PowerPoint and Canva.

CHAPTER 5

Exploring Spiritual Elements of This Journey

I DEBATED WHETHER TO address spirituality in this book. We are all from such diverse backgrounds, I don't think I have the right to tell anyone what to believe. I don't know for sure what the full truth is or what's right, so how could I preach it to anyone else? However, I remember what it felt like to be at rock bottom. It was such a spiritual experience, feeling so isolated and lost and lonely. If you feel that way right now or have any lingering emotions from having felt that way, my hope is that I can be a friend to you by including this chapter.

Here in Trinidad, we have a very diverse population in terms of race and country of origin and therefore we have many, many religions operating side by side. Though I grew up in a home that was Presbyterian (a Protestant Christian religion rooted here by Canadian and Scottish missionaries), I have attended Presbyterian, Hindu, Roman Catholic, Anglican Catholic, Pentecostal, Muslim, Mormon and Interfaith prayer sessions at school, in my home and community, and in my friends' homes. So, although I have often heard people speaking of the one right religion, I feel blessed to be able to see many commonalities in those religions that I do know, and to be able to recognise a universal truth even in religions that are not my own.

There were some heavy existential questions that came up again and again as we went through the protracted experience of Em's birth defects followed by open heart surgery, followed by the bleed out and brain injury, followed by the prognosis of a vegetative state and managing life since then. Some of the big ones included:

1. Has God abandoned us?
2. Is this just a random thing that could have happened to anyone?
3. I was told that if I lived a good life and worked hard, all would be well in my life, so how could this happen to me? Why is life being so unfair to me?
4. Am I being punished for doing something wrong?
5. Is this the result of "bad karma" because I hurt someone else? How terrible a person have I been to have caused this to happen to my child, my family, and me?

Sean and I were talking about the first question just this week. I asked him if, at some point during the past eight years, he ever felt like God abandoned us and he said "yes". Strangely, walking beside Sean through the exact same events, I sometimes felt the opposite. I did not put words to it then, but I felt guided by God on my most broken days. I remember Sean and me sitting on the floor outside of the ICU room with Emma bleeding out fifteen feet in front of us, and codes being trumpeted, and doctors massaging her heart and trying in vain for twenty minutes to restart it, and blood being transfused to her, and alarms blaring discordantly. I had lost hold of any bearing in the world except my husband's hand and, at rock bottom, the only action that flowed to me was to pray. So, Sean and I prayed holding

EXPLORING SPIRITUAL ELEMENTS OF THIS JOURNEY

hands, just letting my intuition determine the prayer that came. I remember something like this was what I said, "God, I know I should be praying to accept your will, and that is what I have prayed up to this point, but I can't say that now. Give me back my child. Please God, give me back my Emma." And immediately, Emma's ECG started beeping and she had come back to us.

I don't know why I never felt angry at God for letting this happen, why I did not perceive it as Him abandoning Emma or us. I guess something within told me that it made no sense to blame God or anyone else because what was done was done, and I needed to focus on survival and recovery. That was genuinely the first conscious decision Sean and I made: not to pursue a lawsuit because all our energy needed to be invested in Emma. I think God was guiding that decision, too.

When my son Bryan was two, he told me of a memory he had of standing with God and being asked which Mommy he wanted, and he chose me. I was amazed because I felt that his story, at that age, was untainted. It planted a seed of joy inside me. Nothing really happened further to that little share, but when Emma was brain injured, I spent many hours across many years asking myself why she was going through this, and what we had done to be trapped in this life that felt like limbo so often. I have felt so much pain about being limited in what we could do together, and unbearably more pain when I berate myself for being so selfish to think "poor me" when it is my precious child who is being subjected to so much every second of every day. And then I look at my "poor child" and 90% of the time she is shining with a joy I have not seen anywhere else except in other special needs children.

And then Bryan's words seem to sprout new meaning for me, and I think, maybe we all chose each other in this family, maybe we chose this life and this experience. Maybe Emma chose this experience and we all agreed to be here to help her through it because there is something to be achieved, some service to give, some learning to be had. I don't think Sean shares exactly these views with me, but as I reflected on what I wanted to write here, I mentioned my thinking to him and he said he respects my views, but has a lot more thinking to do before he can say what meaning or sense he has made of this whole thing.

Now, believing what I have just written doesn't mean I have been able to shrug and say, "Oh well, we chose this," and whistle through our challenges. I'm still wrestling to find meaning. The "we chose this" is comforting to me sometimes, and sometimes it is just so confusing that, figuratively, it whacks me in the face. I mean, who in Heaven's name actually chooses to do this to themselves, right? Why would Emma choose to be severely brain-damaged and trapped in a bed and in pain with two dislocated hips and poor circulation and challenged with sight and speech and mobility and organ functionality? Why would I agree to be party to it? I can get angry at myself for being a fool and choosing this situation, or I can get angry about believing the nonsense about this experience being my choice, or I can get angry at this whole thing being foisted on us intentionally or randomly. Circular thinking from which I can't escape, right?

And then in my lowest times, crying next to Emma, I sometimes just look into her trusting little face, and rub my rough cheek against her downy one and feel such peace flood into me from her. She loves so fully and unconditionally, she believes everyone who interacts with her is caring and generous, she knows (like the sparrow in a hymn when I was a child) that God is providing for her. I am the doubting one, who tries to manage risk, who says we need to plan and save and protect, and so I am the one suffering in each moment while Emma, the one with the brain injury, is radiating Heaven-like grace, peace, and joy.

> I look into Emma's trusting face and rub my cheek against hers and feel such peace flood into me from her.

EXPLORING SPIRITUAL ELEMENTS OF THIS JOURNEY

What Fits You and Your Family

How do you view your situation and your child's situation, my friend, in the context of your own spirituality? Do you relate it to specific lines in a particular religious book? Do you pray and let your intuition guide your thoughts and beliefs? Do you mix and match it all, somewhat as I do? Whatever the case, I hope you find some relief in exploring the questions that come up and make sense of your context in your own unique way.

It is only during this last year that I have learned to accept myself enough to risk sharing my opinion, and thus chose to open my heart and air my views publicly by writing this book. All I can share is what I know, feel, and believe based on what I have learned, observed and experienced. The same is true for you. I say this to you just in case you need to hear it. As long as you are not hurting someone else, the only thing that matters is figuring out your truth and letting that truth shine from you.

What I have found is that what I believe shifts, expands, contracts, morphs constantly as I experience new things, and as I tune in to other people's experiences and stories. Also, I observed some years ago that just because I share the same background and childhood influences as someone else, that is no predictor that we will both have similar spiritual beliefs or practices. For example, I grew up with a right-brained (creative and language-loving) mother and a very left-brained (logical and science-loving) father and went to church almost every week in the village Presbyterian church with many of my extended family members and community-members. I went on to become an engineer, so I had a scientific, proof-oriented approach to most things. My religious practices weren't scientific at all; I

> What I believe shifts, expands, contracts, morphs constantly as I experience new things.

was someone who would "just believe" and I never stopped to think it could be any different than what I had been brought up to believe.

Change came slowly and crept into me unseen over the decades, and then, when Emma became brain-injured, it felt like my spiritual stock-taking was put into a front-line position. When science does not seem to be able to make your daughter's heart beat again and a desperate prayer flips the switch in a micro-second, then it seems to me that the unseen, Universal Energy, Spirit, God is at work.

I hold the view that God lives in me and I am a facet of God's energy. In my logic, based on the first set of text in Genesis of the Bible, "In the beginning…" there was God. So, if only God was there in the empty Universe in the beginning, and if I exist now, then (given the scientific truth that energy can neither be created nor destroyed) it makes sense that my energy is a facet of the One God's energy (not to mention that my intuition tells me I am connected to the whole in an intrinsic way). To round it out, I feel that in the same way that a parent lives within his child, God lives within me, even at the same time that I am a part of the all-encompassing God.

What matters most is coming to your own knowing of what makes sense in this arena for you. There are things you have been taught, experiences you have had, observations you have made, and all of these and more have established your religious and/or spiritual codes and beliefs. Perhaps, as was my experience, your child's special needs have sparked questions or shaken up the order into which your beliefs have been constructed. If you are introspecting and questioning a lot, it can be taxing. It can fill you with doubt, fear, worry, even a sense of failing others if some foundational beliefs are being tested. If you are experiencing tough emotions, I hold space for you; I think this may be one of the most difficult things to face as we make meaning of our child's and our own situation.

For me, there were innumerable useful approaches that brought me hope and insight as I sought to get clear on which way was up, spiritually, and where I fit in the big picture (at least at this current level of my understanding). Chief among these were prayer, gratitude and affirmation practices, meditation, creative endeavours (writing poetry, making art, creating songs, dancing, beginning to intensify my efforts to fulfil what I see as my Soul's purpose), energy work such as Reiki and, recent conversations with my husband and others about our spiritual beliefs and shifts. I talk about some of these in the next section.

Let Your Intuition Guide You

You're a special needs parent. At least most of you reading this book are. You know what it is like to have run out of steam or hope, or to have become so broken by fear, loss, guilt, blame, shame, isolation, or a million other taxing emotions and events. You know what it is like to both literally and figuratively lie on the floor, drained of energy and will and at a loss for what you should do next. When the knowing filters into you and you are able to move to the next step, you may not have been able to say where the knowing was coming from, or how you were functioning, but it may have felt like you were a vessel, or a robot and you were being directed by some silent guide.

This was the guidance, I believe, that helped me through the dark days while Emma was bleeding out and lying comatose, seizing, undergoing x-rays at 2 am night after night, and being diagnosed with severe brain injury. I will always be grateful for that guidance, and to me it still seems Divine. Now when I look back on it, I feel that I was living the sentences of the Footprints poem, because I truly feel that God carried me in those most trying times.

You know what it is like to both literally and figuratively lie on the floor, drained of energy and will and at a loss for what you should do next.

I believe that our intuition has a place in all of our life circumstances, not just the emergency ones. I believe that every time I hear the little voice inside me (while I've expressed mine is at my heart centre, I have heard others say theirs lies in their head or in their gut), that intuitive nudge is the calling or advice of my God-connected Soul. Without that intuitive knowing, where would we be as we try to figure out what our babies need when they cry as newborns? It is our intuition that helps us "just know" they want food or a diaper change or to be turned, burped, sung to, cuddled, or a million other things.

About six months after Em's injury, we were back in Trinidad and being told much the same as those in the USA had said: they did not see hope for her medically, and we'd better get used to life this way. Not having any hope on the medical horizon, we took Em to therapy, but she was throwing up and screaming and having such traumatic reactions to most therapists that it seemed therapy might not be very beneficial either. Desperation may have been what led me inward, because outward solutions were not working.

In my hardest times, prayer provided me with the feeling that I was being supported. I always had someone to talk with, someone that I knew would understand me fully and love me unconditionally. Many of my prayerful conversations with God asked for understanding or faith or hope, for healing for Em, for protection for Sean and Bry, for guidance, solutions, and a myriad of other things, crying and mourning and leaning on Him.

I was not content with just praying, though. I needed to do things to help Em. One of Sean's sisters talked with me about a healing modality called Reiki and I decided to learn it. I began reading more about energy healing and the energy of our bodies. I learned about chakras and chakra balancing. I learned about guided meditation and transmutation meditation. I learned about auras. As I learned, I came to feel more ease with tapping into my intuition. That process

EXPLORING SPIRITUAL ELEMENTS OF THIS JOURNEY

of letting myself listen to my intuition took years, and it is still early days for me.

However, I have to tell you that the biggest stumbling block for me was my reliance on my logic. I am a left-brained, logical, right-handed, traditional engineer. At least that is what might appear on paper. Learning to connect more with my emotions and allow God to lead me when I have been lost has really taken me into a different lane, and so I feel I'm as connected with left brain as right brain now. My advice is not to allow your logical mind to block your ability to commune with your intuition. Both are important parts of you, and both will work together well to help you serve your child while juggling everything else.

So why has it been so important for me to tell you that connecting with my intuition has been my lifeline? Because I have felt such support and hope as I have tapped into my intuition through meditation, visualisation, poetry writing, journaling, and art during the past few years. I have reached a space where (although, sometimes I still feel deep despair and worry)

I start my day with genuine gratitude for both my children and Sean, and especially feel transported watching the love my children have for each other and feeling the constant vortex of joy in which Emma seems to live. Maybe that gratitude has become easier to feel because my visualisations have included (1) me holding Emma's hand and walking on a path through our garden-to-be, and (2) a simple wooden house and a huge garden making up my retreat centre for special needs families, like yours and mine, to whom I feel so connected.

Gratitude and affirmations have helped me to tune in to feeling supported by the Universe. My gratitude practice started with finding small things—a bird twittering or Emma laughing—and feeling my heart light up. There are so many small things I find now to chuckle about or offer silent thanks for. Even when I can't find something to be grateful about on a hard day, I rely on my memory to connect me to gratitude.

Gratitude, in turn, boosts my ability to affirm, because when I feel the Universe provides even small measures of joy and possibility for me, it becomes easier for me to believe that more joy and abundance are available to me. So, I affirm that I have what it takes to create a thriving business, to make a difference to each person I serve, to become healthier and stronger, and I always connect my affirmations to seeing the benefit, because that boosts my motivation and pushes me out of shyness and fear.

Conclusion

So, dear friend, without knowing the specifics of your family's story, I feel certain that your child's special needs play a part in your spiritual point of view. I can tell you that what I have shared is not set in stone for me; it evolves almost daily because there is always so much changing within our family and within our world to force me to re-evaluate my beliefs and shift my behaviours. I expect that you may perceive at least some, and maybe even many, differences between our situations and our thoughts on what I shared in this chapter. Regardless of those differences, I feel connection with you because of the parts of our story that we share—the hurt, the doubt, the love, the joy, and the hope for a better future as we grow emotionally, physically, mentally, and spiritually—because of this journey with our children.

Your Checklist

In case you haven't taken notes, here's a little checklist of the big takeaways from this chapter.

✓ What existential questions are you being drawn into exploring, prompted by your journey with your special needs child? Maybe yours include:
  - ☐ Has God abandoned us?
  - ☐ Was this a random thing that could happen to anyone?
  - ☐ Am I being punished for something?
  - ☐ Could this be a journey we are here to learn/teach something from?

✓ Put your situation into a context that fits you and your family.
  - ☐ If you have a religious book you lean into, what lines give you comfort or insight?
  - ☐ What is your intuition guiding you to believe/think/do?
  - ☐ Figure out your truth and give yourself permission to live in that truth.
  - ☐ Allow yourself the grace to continuously adapt.

✓ Some practices may support you if your own beliefs are being shaken and you are trying to find yourself.
  ☐ Pray.
  ☐ Meditate.
  ☐ Be grateful.
  ☐ Use affirmations.
  ☐ Be creative each day, even if all you can spare is a few minutes.
  ☐ See if an energy practice (e.g., grounding, Reiki) appeals to you.

CHAPTER 6

Shaping At-Home Interventions

REGARDLESS OF WHAT your individual situation is with your child's particular challenges—the country you live in, the state-provided services being delivered right to your house or at a centralised location, the range of medical and therapy services available and accessible—you and your family are likely to feel the desire to support your child's development at home. Many professionals will encourage this, and even provide guidance on what to do and how to do it. In addition, your own intuition will guide you about activities to do with your child. Never discount the value of your own instincts.

This chapter reviews some of the approaches that have made a difference for Emma and all of us in my family. It does share a lot from Emma's experience, and I hope that you might find elements of what you experience with your child in parts of this chapter. Please, take what applies, adapt it to your needs and style, and shelve the rest in case it might reveal relevance later on, as the situation with your child evolves.

Touch and Feel

When Em was first hurt, she was in an ICU recovering from open heart surgery, with tubes into her chest and down her throat. She had been poked and prodded and cut into. Undoubtedly, she was in pain and confused about what was happening to her. After the brain injury, she transitioned to being in a coma, and it was hard to discern the degree to which she emerged from that coma, because she had lost all her senses and her ability to suck and swallow. She continued to be poked and prodded all through the weeks that followed her incident.

As she regained her ability to feel physical sensations, we began seeing tears on Emma's cheeks. Though her mouth would open and close, no sounds came out, because she was mute. It was heart-breaking to see our child locked inside a silent body, while surrounded by other ICU rooms where children were calling for their parents.

In much the same way that parents learn to use their intuition to decide if their baby's cry is a cry for a diaper change or for food, or to be held, or because pain is being felt, we let our intuition guide us. Emma was being subjected to a lot of impersonal touch, since innumerable tests and checks were conducted, and tubes and needles put in and taken out of her. I read somewhere that because pain so often followed touch for her, she might begin experiencing fear and dread whenever she was touched.

I realise now that all that was being done to her was such an invasion of her personal space and lack of respect and consideration of her own will, and often it would happen without even the courtesy of a word to let her know something was about to be done. As her ability to make a sort of truncated scream emerged, we recognised that touch was indeed causing Em a lot of pain, so we set out to change that.

We began learning about two kinds of touch: deep pressure massage, and a lighter stroking touch. The light touch was unbearably painful to Emma in the beginning and would make her cry. I made a connection between what Emma was physically feeling and the way we can turn a knob on a radio to turn up or turn down sound. It appeared that her nerves just at surface-skin level were able to feel sensation, but in an overwhelming way. We needed to find a way to turn down the "volume" there. On the other hand, it appeared that her ability to feel deeper touch sensations was negligible and so we needed to be able to turn up the "volume" in that regard.

We started by changing how we touched Emma, believing it would not be forever. We shifted as far as possible to deep touch. No more short, light movements against her skin; instead, we followed her baths with firm, long massaging strokes as we applied creams. We would cup our hands around her arm or leg and squeeze our way up and down the length of the limb, avoiding squeezing the joints. That deep pressure massage came to be extremely satisfying for her, and she enjoys it to this day, though over time, the pressure we apply has reduced, since she feels sensations with considerably less pressure now.

The most amazing deep pressure activity we did was one where we would squeeze her fingertips one by one as hard as we could (between our own first finger and thumb) until she stiffened or made a sound. That would indicate that she had felt the sensation in her deep nerves. Let me assure you that we were not hurting Emma, our pressure was applied only until she felt the pressure, and we'd then stop and move to the next finger. Now (eight years later) when I do the exercise with Emma, she is able to feel the sensation before I apply very much pressure at all, and she typically laughs and pulls her hand away.

The other thing we noticed early on was that Emma disliked whenever anyone interacted with her mouth. I would put this little finger cap on my index finger and clean her teeth and tongue each day, and I realised that the activity seemed to cause her pain or significant discomfort when I was working around her tongue and upper palate. At that stage, I became the only one she would tolerate with her mouth ablutions, and I noticed that if I removed the finger cap and just used my finger, her stress reduced. The feel of the plastic material against her skin was abhorrent to her.

With the shift to using my finger in her mouth, the exercise changed. It became not just about completing a task I had to do *to* Emma, but about an opportunity to interact *with* Emma and be gentle and loving to her. My finger was no longer being put into her mouth to efficiently wipe and brush. Mouth-cleaning activities became a favourite activity for Emma after a while. When I said, "palate now," she would open up and allow me access to her palate, and with every part of her mouth that I named, she would be cued in to where I was going next, so she was prepared for the shift of my finger. No longer foisted on her, the activity became something that we did together and enjoyed. Although medical people doubted that Emma was receiving language for years despite our reports of that being the case, Emma's ability to understand "ok, front teeth now," or "let's do the back teeth", or "don't bite, Em" were all indicators of her growing ability to understand and respond to our language cues. We thought it was pretty cool that our touch interventions were leading into language reception skills for her.

The recognition that Em did not like the plastic finger cap in her mouth helped us start exploring the way that different materials feel against our skin. That was such an important realisation in supporting Emma's recovery. We tried many different materials stroked against Emma's skin. Sometimes she would tolerate materials against her palm and fingers (terrycloth) but hated them against her arms. We used a range of materials to just work on growing her exposure and teaching her contrasting textures. For example, gritty sandpaper, velvety ears on her plush stuffed animal, knobbly seersucker, dry and tough cardboard, light and crinkly crêpe paper, cloudlike pompoms and cotton balls, plush tassels, a rough bath glove, a squishy rubber ball, hard and smooth plastic, meshy tulle, the ropey braid of her doll, woven cotton cloth, hard and cool metal, a cold squishy gel pack, and the list goes on.

Bowel Movements/Gut Motility

Emma's brain injury stopped her from being able to move and a direct consequence was a change in her motility. Constipation was such a big problem that often ten days would go by with no bowel movement (BM) from her, so her tummy would be hard and bloated, and she would be dealing with discomfort and pain. We leaned on medical practitioners and tried a range of remedies (prunes, prune purees and prune juice were the first thing, but we also tried syrup of figs, orvilax, lactulose, and many other medical products) to address the issue by softening stool, increasing mucus production, or increasing water directed to the lower end of the colon. Some of these worked, but they would only work for a short time before she built up a tolerance and we were back to square one. In the case of one particular product, Miralax, Em has not seemed to build up a tolerance, and we use 1/3 dose most days, just to give her some support without using so much that she becomes fully dependent on the medicine.

We also tried adapting her food. Spinach was good for her nutrition, but we found it constipated her (likely due to the high iron content). Surprisingly, banana also constipated her, so we stopped giving her banana for several years, even though she loved it. I should mention that we tried water, but Emma still has difficulty swallowing water (the thinnest liquid) so it would take more than an hour for her to drink 2 oz. of water (1/4 glass), and so water-drinking was only a part of the plan to hydrate her. Hydration also had to take place through the food she ate. One God-sent solution for us came when we gave Emma her first taste of mango. Her mouth would open so wide and so fast for another bite that we couldn't serve her fast enough. We began giving her a mango a day, when in season, and that improved the situation. Unfortunately, mangoes were not always available, and so constipation has remained a concern in our lives, though much less a challenge than before.

The most terrible fall-back for me was (only when we were well into a second week without a bowel movement) to administer a laxative. In the beginning, we used a paraffin suppository administered anally, which would trigger her lower colon to move and cause a BM in a matter of minutes. Worried that the capsule could have unknown side effects, I only administered half of the suppository. It worked (and rapidly) but I did not like that she screamed and cried for hours afterward. Again, my intuition guided me, and I decided to try a suppository on myself. Although the efficacy was great, I experienced gut-wrenching cramps that made me writhe in pain for two days afterward. I had been assured there would be no side effects on Em, but my own experience with the product showed me that I needed to leave no stone unturned as I evaluated options to help Em. We never used suppositories again.

Emma would be waiting so long between the BMs that her stool was large and hard, and as she passed it, she would bleed. The pressure her body was under brought on worsening of her hernia situation. She had a hernia right under the sternum incision (where I always felt the doctors maybe neglected to put in one last stitch) and with all the crying, her intestines would push up through the space and balloon under the skin of her chest. Several more hernias emerged around her navel area, and these would bulge when she cried, especially with the pain of BMs.

The motility issue became so severe that we began using enemas, but only in times of extreme need. Within minutes of administering the enema liquid, Emma would begin screaming and would pass the impacted stool, but often she would vomit during the event, and it would leave her drained and listless. We felt like we were living in a warzone, with all the mental and physical strain, and the emotional hardship of not only hearing and seeing our child suffering daily and bleeding regularly, but worse, making the decision to administer these drugs to her that would exacerbate her pain and suffering before she could get relief.

We were really motivated to figure out how to bring Emma past her pain. Even the most empathetic doctors would end their message of compassion followed by a shrug, admitting there was nothing they could do to help Emma reduce her pain without drugs, and that pain relieving drugs might just reduce the responsiveness of her gut. Plus, Emma would likely lose efficacy in gut function as she would develop dependence on the enema for evacuation.

Not knowing what else to do, I began searching the internet for alternatives. For the first time, I was willing to try holistic approaches, and acupressure and reflexology came up as options that we decided to try. I started with acupressure. It was not invasive; all I had to do was press certain points and they were supposed to help Emma's gut become more relaxed, or maybe it was that it would trigger peristalsis, which is the contracting movement of the gut that pushes stool along the intestine to evacuation. The four points that worked well for us (maybe there are more but I remember these and still use these because they work) were pressing with my index finger pad against (1) the inner side of her elbow joint(s), (2) the inner side of her knee joints and squeezing lightly with my thumb and forefinger (3) between her thumb and first finger bones and (4) between her big and first toe(s). Although these worked, they did not work as well as we wanted, and so we kept looking for more ways to help Emma.

That's when I found a reflexology diagram for the sole of the foot. (See "Appendix A" on page 177.) I learned that we could gently rub the soles of Em's feet following a smooth path resembling the upside-down U of our colon and actually trigger movement of the stool along the colon followed by opening of the anus to allow evacuation. To those who think this may be too good to be true, I totally get your scepticism; I doubted it once, too. The evidence that it works is that Em typically has a BM every one to two days now.

One extra tip to boost motility is to get your child moving. Doctors say we should let them walk or run or jump. Emma, in the beginning years, could not move her legs much at all, so none of that was possible. Sound and music changed that.

Sound and Music

The absolute biggest game changer in opening up vistas for Em has been sound and music.

Music helped her hearing to re-emerge right after the brain injury, we started to play classical CDs every moment that she was awake. Over time, we found that when the music came on, she would turn her head toward the music.

One of the first approaches to helping Em to find pleasure was to sing nursery rhymes to her. I grew up with my mom singing an endless repertoire of them, and I had continued the tradition with my son and nephews. So, doing it for Em was natural, although sometimes I would feel sad because she could not sing along with me. It was obvious that they soothed her and gave her pleasure as I held her in my arms and rocked her in the rocking chair or lay next to her on the bed. Over time, Emma's ability began emerging so she could move her hands and feet a little, and that lit me up as she became able to show enthusiasm about her nursery rhymes and the little songs I made up for her. From there, we added action poems to the routine, and "BINGO", "Row, Row, Row Your Boat," and "Incy Wincy Spider" became my ways to get her involved in intentional movement and relaxation of her hyperextended arms and legs. She would enjoy herself so much that she never felt it was work or therapy.

Nursery rhymes also provided an opening for us to support Emma to initiate sound on her own. We made up a nightly routine, based on an animal sound puzzle we bought for her. The actual animal sounds from the puzzle scared her, making her startle and cry. Instead, we would talk to her about the animals in turn and ask each other and her "What does the doggie (or other animal) say?" and each of us take a turn to make an animal sound until we had exhausted all the animals from the puzzle. Then we would say, "Well, Emma Lucy, it's time to go to sleep. Which animal do you think is going to say good night tonight?" and we would wait until she made the sound of her choice. It didn't matter if her sound actually sounded like the actual animal sound (Em mostly says "ah" with different degrees of loudness). What mattered was that she responded audibly. We'd then cheer, and she would laugh joyfully along with us.

Sound can be used as a cue. If Emma spaced out (she used to have regular seizures), I might snap my fingers or sing a note to help her focus again. Sound can also be a celebration. We start each day with gratitude and prayer on Em's bed. It ends with the singing of a threefold Amen that she has recently started to sing with us, in her own way. There is nothing more joyful to me than hearing Em's laugh and attempt to sing on her own, as I remember when she could not even make a sound when she was in pain in the ICU.

Em's musical taste also became evident over time. Several years ago, I brought a music player into her room to try to give Sean some mental relaxation. He had certain favourites and Emma eventually would laugh in delight when the first strains of certain songs began. It got to the point where she would not go to sleep until we played a certain group of pop songs for her. When we sang her nursery rhymes, she would not be satisfied and settle down to be put to sleep. We had to let her hear John Legend's "All of Me", Passenger's "Let Her Go",

Aviici's "Hey Brother", and Imagine Dragons' "Counting Stars" before she would relax and allow her dad to rock her to sleep. Now that we know Em actually has musical tastes, we have built playlists for her. In addition to the others mentioned, she enjoys music ranging from "Incy Wincy Spider" to "Sing" by The Carpenters to Ed Sheeran to nursery rhymes and Christmas carols.

Music and sound have also helped Emma build up tolerance to certain noises. For example, Emma would be so terrified by the high-pitched sound of the rain or sirens that she would startle, scream, and cry until she threw up. That negative reaction would disrupt whatever she was doing, and her hearing of high-pitched sound was so acute that long after we had stopped hearing a siren, she would still have hitched breathing and her arms thrown out in alarm. We worked on this by exposing Emma to the sound of a rain stick in small doses, and we also turned rain time into fun by singing songs about the rain. "Rain, Rain, Go Away," is still one of her favourites.

Recently, I learned from a singer friend, Monifa Harris, about a vocal exercise I could do to try to develop my ability to sing. It was to make a siren sound. I did the siren a few times and the next day as I was playing with Em, my intuition led me to try it with Em. To my amazement, Emma was highly engaged and began taking turns with me to make the siren sound. I was floored at the variation in tone that she was able to produce! What we were seeing was Emma's ability to take turns, to mimic a sound, and to learn a new skill. All evident in a five-minute exercise that she had been exposed to *once*.

Taste and Mouthfeel

We also did some work on Emma's ability to taste and enjoy textures in her mouth. In earlier years, we were just working to try to get her to swallow a drop or two of almond milk. (We stopped cow's milk after learning that milk increases mucus production, and also learning that bedridden people are more likely to develop pneumonia than other people because the fluid just settles and collects in their lungs.) She used to be fed by way of a gastrostomy tube until we supported her, against all odds, to a point where she once again learned to swallow (she has never learned to suck very well) thick liquids. She was able to swallow the almond milk and thicker water (i.e. coconut water) and thinned purees, and with effort could swallow plain water before we removed the gastrostomy tube entirely.

Once the tube feeding days were behind us, we set out to develop her ability to eat more textures and types of food. The secret to that, we found, was stimulating her sense of taste. We would cut very ripe mangoes into strips. She began to bite soft bits that crushed as her palate closed on them and then swallow them. We would boil root vegetables such as sweet potatoes as well as ripe plantains and crush these as a base. We could add carrots or peas or other veggies to give her a variety of tastes and nutrients. One thing she loved was callaloo, a delicious local "soup" made from boiled leaves of the taro root (dasheen leaves) crushed together with pumpkin and coconut milk. Emma also loved fish and crushed broccoli and various crushed savoury bean dishes early on; the strong flavours appeared to entrance her, maybe because they could be picked up better than mild flavours by her sense of taste, which was then only just emerging.

We taught Em to chew better by using crunchy foods. We would give her a bit of cookie and she would crunch down and laugh, then work hard to get the cookie bite back between her teeth to hear another laugh-inducing crunch. Similarly, icing or jam on her lips were encouragement for her to try to lick her lip to get more of the sweet taste. We learned to always be on the lookout for her unexpected and interesting responses to something we did by chance.

As years passed, we were able to move Em to biting into green beans and chewing rice (soft boiled) and even eating scrambled eggs and pasta salads. She loves boiled eggs when they are cubed in an avocado and tomato salad.

Movement and Colour

It is said that sight is the sense that boosts learning and development the most in children. Em has been diagnosed as blind and so that was a big cause for concern for us. No matter what sensory limitations our children have, it is our job to find out what sensory abilities they do have. Those sensory abilities are the doors through which we can communicate with them and help them learn and develop.

> Sensory abilities are the doors through which we can communicate with them and help them learn and develop.

I cannot encourage you enough to offer your child stimulation in areas where their sensory ability has been diagnosed as not present or low. As you can tell from the earlier sections, we relied primarily on touch and sound, and as Em's ability to taste developed, we have incorporated activities around eating (taste and smell). But even in the area where she was diagnosed as having no ability, we have seen some improvement, because we have continued to give her exposure and stimulation.

Although Em has been diagnosed as blind, we read about a condition called cortical visual impairment and asked about it because we believed she did show a light response and some sign of being able to track that light. We were berated by the ophthalmologist we first went to; she said Em was tracking our sound, because we were doing our evaluations of tracking poorly. She insisted Em was blind and that would not change, so we should stop wasting our time.

We decided to still use the internet to learn about what we could do for a child with cortical visual impairment, and we began working with her by moving a small light side to side and up and down in front of her face. We also did the same with bright red items and, later, bright yellow items on a black background (for contrast). A few years later, Em is now able to track these enough that we know she is definitely NOT blind. We have also strung Christmas lights around the top of two walls of Em's room and when those are turned on, it is such a joy to watch her eyes flicker side to side at the movement of the blue and white flashing lights. I suspect it may be only the white light that she sees, but the fact remains that SHE SEES!

Understanding how sight development happens in babies was important. Children first see contrast between black and white. After that, sight development continues starting with red (longest wavelength of light) and moving to yellow and on according to the colours of the rainbow (cool memory aid). We have appealed to Em's growing ability to see by using plain black and white board books and a few fancier versions of those board books with foil inserts in shiny gold and red. This Christmas, our gift to Em was a binder full of homemade sensory cards with various colours and textures to encourage her colour perception and ability to locate items with her fingers.

We have a long way to go in this area, but we are hopeful because any progress, as we have seen elsewhere in her sensory development, means that more progress is possible.

Activities to Target Multiple Senses

In more recent years, we have been playing with combining texture, sound, and even taste, by extending Em's exposure in many ways. We watch her face scrunch up as she evaluates cold, squishy, tangy yogurt on her tongue, and wait for the recognition of a taste she enjoys, followed by her open mouth demanding more. We drag her hand through dry, smooth, uncooked red beans and let her feel the hardness and hear it swishing around against a bowl. We tell her to lift her hand to communicate to us if she wants another mouthful of something good or if she wants another line of a song. We call on her to instruct us to stack squeezable rubber stacking blocks and hard plastic stacking blocks one by one, then challenge her to find the tower and knock it down. We watch to see if she responds differently to the soft thud of the soft blocks as compared to the jarring knock of the hard plastic ones, or if the softer feel under her fingers is preferred by her to the smooth, hard plastic. We build her proprioception (ability to sense her own body in space) by rocking her in different positions in a hammock, rocking her on our lap in a rocking chair, taking her on a "horsey ride" as she sits on my walking or galloping lap, and holding her in our arms and spinning around either on our feet or in a chair on wheels.

A lovely idea for multi-sensory stimulation is to create activities in stages, when your child can handle longer activities. For example, we might read a story (or make up a story) about a spider, then sing "Incy Wincy Spider" and do the actions for the action poem as we sing, then do a craft activity including an opportunity for Em to feel the rough pipe cleaner legs of the spider and see the craft by making it in only two contrasting colours (e.g., red on a black or a white background). Em has learned cause-and-effect from Incy Wincy playtime because we start crawling our fingers from her feet and she laughs because she knows our version will end in tickling at her neck. This past month, I've been stomping on our wood floor as I walk up to her in the bed. She laughs uproariously because she knows the "big fat spider" will crawl up her torso and tickle her neck very soon after the stomping begins. That's helping her with her cause-and-effect logic.

The very best integrative activities are those where we take Emma out of the house. They take a lot of effort and we wish we could do them much more often, because of the value we see for her. There have been visits to parks to sit under trees on benches or on a thin sheet and listen to the birds and put feet on grass and sing songs and laugh. On my birthday, I often request to go to the Pointe-a-Pierre Wildfowl Trust where we have a family membership, so Emma can join us in appreciating nature's beautiful flora and fauna, including lotus flowers and our national bird, the scarlet ibis.

Every year since 2014, we have made at least one multi-day trip to the beach. Due the Coronavirus outbreak, 2020 was the only year we missed the tradition. Part of the experience is sitting with Em on our lap and allowing the waves to tickle at our toes as we get her accustomed to the high-pitched swish of the waves, which discombobulates her. Then we rub her feet against the gritty, wet sand and let the waves splash her. Finally, we sit further into the surf, where we get a little rough treatment from the waves and warn her when a wave is about to hit. In 2019, we had the joy of seeing Emma laugh in the waves for the first time. I still feel such joy suffuse me as I remember that precious sound; how good success felt after five years of trying and trying and hoping and believing that change would come.

I would be remiss if I did not point out how critical socialisation has been for Emma's holistic development. About four years ago, no kindergarten schools were willing to let us bring Em in to have the opportunity to interact with other children. However, along with Em's early intervention therapist, we were convinced this sort of interaction would help Em learn to cope better with being outside of our home, handling unexpected noises, and making social connections with others. We decided to approach Rochelle's E.C.C.E., the preschool Bryan had attended, as a last effort. We were invited to bring Em in to meet them in person. How shocked and grateful we were to receive an email that day, saying they would welcome us to bring Em to spend time with them whenever we wanted and at no charge.

Em loved every moment at Rochelle's. Students came over to join us at our table to hold Em's hand and say good morning and play with Em's toys and read books with us, teachers led the whole school assembly in singing Em's favourite songs, and she would laugh in delight. Em had the opportunity to stroke a dog that came in for career day with a Vet. Em would join everyone in the play park to use the slides and swings, and there were at least two occasions when Em even joined the annual Carnival jump-up decked out in her own costume! These were not just people providing a service; these were people who lived in love and it translated to Em's experiences and her development.

On one occasion, Em was sick and unable to go to school for an extended period. The first years were making a hand-print painting as a gift to one of the staff, and I received a call to say they could not complete the piece without Em's handprint. Em belonged to no class; no teacher had her on their roll, and yet they remembered my little girl. That fills me with such gratitude even up to today that I am crying as I write this. Isn't that what we all want: to be accepted and loved? The years at Rochelle's helped Emma to love car rides and interactions with others, and to tolerate the unpredictable noises of the real world (after several weeks she would not bat an eye at the excited screams and laughter and crying that typify preschool sounds) without having a meltdown.

Right now, we are creating a little sensory garden to appeal to all Em's senses. We already have some bright red and yellow and pink and orange and white flowers, as well as leaves that vary from light and dark green to white and silvery and coloured ones. We have a range of textures on plants, including velvety, prickly, waxy, serrated-edged, and smooth-edged. We have colourful fruits and vegetables including bananas, eggplants, tomatoes, sweet peppers, and ochroes (okra). Some scented herbs are present too, including thyme, rosemary, mint, and chives. A variety of leaf shapes and sizes happens too, for example with large banana leaves and tiny mint and thyme leaves.

> Em belonged to no class; no teacher had her on their roll, and yet they remembered my little girl.

Undoubtedly, I have left several activities out of this chapter because I've forgotten some of the things we've tried with Em over the years because there are too many to capture, due to space limitations. I have tried to give quite a range, though, and I hope they will spark some ideas about how you can create opportunities for developmental play and learning with your child based on your observations of his/her responses as you try new things, or as you see changes in the response given to things tried before.

Medical Care and Other Professional Services

What I have not focused much on has been medical care. That is because I am not a medical doctor and so I cannot say what to do and what to avoid for any child. I do, however, want to mention a few things that I have strong opinions about.

Number one: when choosing a doctor, finding one who has experience and competence is important, but just as important is finding one who has hope and warmth toward your child and you. Being seen and treated as worthy of care and love has made a huge difference to our own ability to hope and to dare and to persevere, and to Em's positivity as she fights her fight.

Number two: don't let "what we do around here" be the limit on what you are considering for your child. We were told by that first ophthalmologist that we should just accept Em's blind diagnosis and relegate our child to a life of darkness. That did not sit right, given what we were observing in our own child. We then went to another well-recognised ophthalmologist who agreed that there is no practice of

> *Don't let "what we do around here" be the limit on what you are considering for your child.*

diagnosing Cortical Visual Impairment in this country, but who did say that Em's optic nerve was pink, indicating she was not blind and there was hope for development of her sight. He told us to go ahead with our at-home interventions if we wanted and see if her sight might improve. Not much hope, I know, but some hope was better than none.

As for Em's oxygen-deprivation-caused (hypoxic) brain injury, I became aware that in some other countries, there are interventions that some children receive in a short window after the injury. Em did not receive these interventions; they were not suggested to us and our research did not raise them for us early enough in her timeline. However, perhaps speaking with a paediatric neurologist and other doctors would let you know what emerging techniques could help your child. I'm hearing people speak of the value of oxygen therapy, and maybe even stem cell therapy.

It also bears mentioning to get a good Paediatric Dentist for your child. Sometimes, medicines can affect teeth, and I suspect this happened with Em, because her teeth were brittle and chipped easily. The first dentist we took her to was impersonal and unempathetic, not a good fit for us. We finally settled at a dentist[1] who answered our questions, patiently explained how to work around Em's challenges, and set up treatment plans to help reduce the tooth damage we were seeing.

I have come to believe in holistic care, and some doctors have a team that rounds out traditional medical care with traditional therapy like Speech, Occupational and Physical therapy, and other services such as Reiki, Osteopathy, ABM, light therapy, TENS treatment, vibration, massage, acupressure, music therapy, and more. Every one of these approaches have positive effects on Em. Additional services that I have heard of special needs children being served by include neuro-chiropractor, MNRI, therapy laser services, infrared heat

---

1 Dr. Annie Kowlessar of Kiddie Care Dental
https://kiddie-care-dental.business.site/

therapy, aromatherapy, and even neuro-acupuncture services offered by trained and certified professionals.

Don't forget to ask about equipment that can promote recovery, prevent decline, increase comfort, and more. Think about mats to increase stimulation during tummy time, adapted wheelchairs/strollers/activity chairs/bath chairs, supports and braces and padding to maintain body support and prevent twisting and deformation, pommels to separate legs and prevent scissoring and dislocation (as happened to Em), and even hoists to lift your child safely (for them and for you). If you can't afford something, you may have to find a temporary substitute until you can save enough or find funding or a hand-me-down. Substitutes won't always be possible, but necessity is the mother of invention, as they say. We have had trouble accessing ankle-foot orthotics (AFOs) and used rigid high-top sneakers as a stand-in in the past. We've rolled up towels to prop Em into an upright position and keep her back from twisting to the side. You might look silly with all the bags you walk around with, but if your child is safer, do it.

Also, don't forget that nutrition is critical for your child's recovery as well. Natural sources are preferred to supplements, but if the natural form is impossible or difficult to access or administer, lean into supplements. Find people who understand the issue your child is facing and get advice from people who are trained and experienced in nutrition. Many doctors may not feel as sure about this aspect. Some of the nutrients we focus on would be Vitamin C, zinc, vitamin D, omega 3, magnesium, and calcium. The last two, we have learned, reduce muscle cramping. Also, remember that nutrition is not always what we add to our child's food; it can also be what we remove. You may find it useful to consider removing dairy (dairy increases mucous production and increases risk of fluid build-up in lungs especially in bedridden people), reducing sugar (for more balanced blood sugar and better functioning of the pancreas, we have learned), and reducing gluten (for less bloating and intestinal discomfort in some people) to start.

There is no substitute for reading and researching widely to understand what is happening with your child and what else could make a difference. Always remember that doctors might be experts in their areas of specialisation, but your job is to be the expert in your child's situation. Please, if some question or doubt comes up in your mind, do not let anyone make you feel stupid about asking it. A doctor who shuts you up or puts you down may be the wrong doctor to rely on. Remember that our doctors are being paid for the service they are providing and no matter how dependent on them you might be, you deserve respect, explanations, answers, and empathy.

Also remember that doctors often give advice based on the accepted practice and what is known as the truth based on their profession's experience. If my child has gotten the prognosis of a vegetative state for life (she was) because only 0.0001% of people in her situation ever get past a vegetative state, then I have to decide if I will accept that declaration, if I will seek a second opinion, and if I might want to fight for my child to be the 0.0001%.

We decided that we would fight because Em was fighting to stay alive, and she deserved whatever we could give to support her in that fight. We are by no means the only parents fighting for our special needs child. I am sure you are too. Lots of doctors and other professionals have built practices to support your fight. Go find them.

Your Checklist

This chapter has focused on structuring approaches to integrate your child's senses into activities that encourage development through pure enjoyment. Here are some approaches and extra tips, related to what has been shared above.

✓ Observe your child's abilities with all the five senses and think about how you can make development and learning fun.
  ☐ Keep a record of your child's current abilities with each sense.
  ☐ Record your child's sensory abilities every so often, so you can see evidence of changes/improvements over time.
  ☐ Keep reading and learning because that must happen for you to get more ideas to support your child's development.
  ☐ Let your logic and your intuition guide you as you devise activities to do with your child.
  ☐ Feel free to check in with a therapist or other specialist on any recommendations made in this chapter. Learning more is always beneficial.

✓ Involve your child in activities and let them be a joyful experience you both share.
  ☐ Have a positive attitude because what your child experiences is directly connected.

- ☐ Observe what activities give your child joy and adapt therapy accordingly.
- ☐ Be sure to consider safety when devising activities for your child.
- ☐ Tell your child what you are doing and give him/her feedback and encouragement.
- ☐ If your child laughs when doing activities, that is to be celebrated! Never think development always needs to feel like work (though sometimes it can be challenging or painful, too).

✓ Incorporate touch-based activities.
- ☐ Observe how well your child feels and enjoys light stroking touch.
- ☐ Observe how well your child is able to feel deep pressure (only squeeze just enough for your child to feel the pressure so you do not hurt them).
- ☐ Use different materials to expose your child to various textures.
- ☐ You can teach your child some opposites using texture contrasts.

✓ Incorporate sight-based activities.
- ☐ Never shine a bright light directly into your child's eye as you can damage their eyesight.
- ☐ Use cards, books, toys, and everyday items to encourage sight and tracking.
- ☐ Start with exposure to black and white.

- ☐ Add red and yellow and work your way to the next colour in the rainbow, as your child develops the ability to see the previous colour.

✓ Incorporate hearing-based activities.
  - ☐ If your child loves a seasonal song, it does not need to stop when the season passes. We sang happy birthday and "Deck the Halls" almost daily to Em in 2020.
  - ☐ A good night activity like singing together or reading/telling a bedtime story can incorporate sound.
  - ☐ For some children, you may be able to do an activity that appeals to their imagination, with everyone taking turns to add a sentence as the family build a story together.
  - ☐ Sound can be used as a cue: if Emma spaces out, I might snap my fingers or sing a note to help her focus again.
  - ☐ Sound can be a celebration: let your child participate in celebrations through singing, humming, or using musical instruments, if they are able.
  - ☐ Be patient and positive: your child may not be able to do something or do it as well as you want right now, but the ability may develop over time and with more exposure and practice.

- ☐ Sometimes, our child's ability can regress. I've seen this in Emma as she shifts to develop some other ability. Be sure to let your doctor know if this happens, but it is par for the course for our journey.

✓ Incorporate smell- and taste-based activities.
- ☐ Smell and taste don't always have to be paired but it is convenient to pair them when activities involve food.
- ☐ Consider stimulating smell and taste by setting up a small sensory garden.

✓ Devise activities that combine multiple senses if your child can handle this increased level of stimulation.
- ☐ You can build wonderful integrative sensory activities around action poems like "Incy Wincy Spider".
- ☐ A lovely idea for multi-sensory stimulation is to create activities in stages, when your child can handle longer activities.
- ☐ A trip to a destination like a beach or park can appeal to many senses, if your child will not be too drained by the trip, or if you can overnight so your child gets enough rest.
- ☐ Social interactions are amazing opportunities for holistic development and sensory integration.

SHAPING AT-HOME INTERVENTIONS

✓ Find the right professionals and keep learning.
  ☐ Find doctors and dentists who fit your child's needs and your own.
  ☐ Expect respect and quality service from the doctors and other professionals who serve you.
  ☐ Round out the care your child receives with holistic services, as appropriate.
  ☐ Provide nutrition to bolster your child's recovery. What will you add and what will you remove? How can sources be natural as far as possible?
  ☐ Research medical interventions, supplementary/holistic services, and equipment that will boost your child's recovery, reduce their risk/decline, and increase their comfort.

I must stress that, in this chapter, I mention only some approaches, and a myriad of others exist out there that I either did not remember to list, don't have experience with, or don't know about yet. I continue to learn about more approaches by joining brain injury communities, attending courses, and reading journals and books in the field, and I encourage you to do the same.

CHAPTER 7

Supporting Your Other Children

I KNOW MANY PARENTS who have other children in addition to their special needs child. Some (including us) had children before their special needs child and chose to have no more afterward. Others had the special needs child first and went on to plan subsequent children, for many reasons including the search for added support for their first child, and the continuation of the love in their family.

There are many single parents who are doing superhuman services caring for their special needs child and other siblings too. Also, there are some amazing people who spread love and joy by fostering or adopting special needs children. I am in awe of those people, and I feel my heart swell with gratitude when I hear stories of this sort of loving-kindness.

My perspective comes from my situation where Sean and I had five very loving years spent with Bryan before Em was born. We decided to try for a second child because we felt Bry was lonely, and he repeatedly asked for a sibling. Em came to us immediately, and Bry was the one who told me I was pregnant. I confirmed the pregnancy a few weeks after his diagnosis! Now, while I could talk about Em's birth at this point, I will not. This is the chapter where I get to shine a light on our other children, who are so special in their own wondrous ways. I am sharing a few different ideas in this chapter, in hope that you will find one or two that could help make things easier, more effective, or more fun for you and your other children.

I should indicate that I am often referring to our other child as he/him. This choice was made to avoid any confusion when I also refer to Em in the text, as she/her will remain distinct.

Never Enough Time

Do you agree that time is at a premium for us? Even before I had any children, it felt like I was always strapped for time; time felt like my most fleeting resource. Then came Bryan and I reorganised my tasks to add studying the developmental stages, singing songs, saying nursery rhymes, reading to (and later with) him, running and playing, doing art and craft (messy craft as he called it with relish as I cringed, thinking about the clean-up!), making charts, and playing board games and outdoor games. It was tiring but very fulfilling for both Sean and me.

When I got pregnant with Em, I was five years older and just starting a job in a whole new industry. I was not as energetic as I wished because starting at a university demanded many extra hours to develop materials for all of my classes. In addition, a five-year-old boy has lots of energy and demands and that stretched me, along with the pregnancy. By the time Em was due, I was wondering how I could juggle the demands of my job and a new baby and still be able to give Bry a good dose of the uncompromised attention he'd had from us since he'd been born. I was concerned he would feel neglected and sidelined, and perhaps even jealous and resentful of Em for taking us away from him.

How do you feel about the availability of time in your situation? Have you found ways to manage time better? Maybe you are burning the candle at both ends, just forcing yourself to get everything done. With the insight I have gleaned from eight years of experience, I caution you to find balance in how you plan and use your time. We will talk about some specifics as the chapter proceeds.

Confusing Emotions

Em being born with Tetralogy of Fallot (4 problems in her heart which would lead to the need for open heart surgery within a matter of months) exacerbated the situation, and we tried to include Bry in our activities by letting him hold her in the rocking chair and involving him as we sang and prayed and planned. Underlying it for me was always a feeling of sadness because I felt I had lost the innocent times I used to spend with Bryan. I felt that he was, at five, having to suddenly grow up.

There were also feelings of resentment, anger, self-judgment—oh, the list goes on and on—because there was no one clear correct path to take when it came to including Bry in what was happening with Emma. As the weeks and months passed, Em was deteriorating. Sean and I decided we would not hide Em's condition from Bry. From our reading we knew that the outcome of surgery would not be certain, and we wanted him to make the most of the time and love he shared with his sister. We shared what Em was facing medically, explained about the surgery and how it would help her, prayed together for God to help us accept what was to come, and spent a lot of time singing and just being together.

We were judged for our open approach, with some extended family members disapproving of us "laying the heavy truth" on Bryan. We went into the surgery explaining the intervention and the risk to him, and we took him with us to the USA for the open-heart surgery. I am glad we took him with us, instead of leaving him behind with my sister's family, because I can't imagine how he would have felt to be on the other side of the phone as Emma flatlined and the brain injury journey began.

We were stuck in the USA with Em in a coma and in rehab for around two months. I think it was after the brain injury that Bryan would have felt the biggest shift in our interaction with him. Suddenly, we were caught up in hoping for Emma's survival, hoping for a sign that a single one of her senses was flickering back to life. We were deciding to have surgery done to insert a feeding (gastrostomy) tube into Emma's tummy. And Bryan was being cared for more often through automaticity than intentionality in many of the hours of each day. We were stressed, numb, crying, worrying, reading, learning, forcing ourselves to eat, doing respiratory therapy and massage, singing and fake laughing for Bryan's sake and our own sake too.

Bry was watching it all with wise, all-seeing eyes at age five. We did not know it then, but he was deciding that we were under stress and he had to grow up and become a responsible caretaker of us, his parents, because he could not cause any more hardship in our lives. We had to wait another several years before we learned that this was the weight he had taken onto his young shoulders.

> At age five, Bry decided he had to grow up and become a responsible caretaker of us, his parents.

When Em reached age three or four, Sean and I began renting a beach house for three days every year. We would take Bry and Em to the beach and use a pool on the resort compound. Our purpose was to give Bry a chance for play and frolicking instead of being locked in our heavy vibe all the time. The second aim was to see if we could do some water-therapy with Em, getting her used to the noise of the surf (which scared her terribly) and giving her a chance to learn to kick her legs, encouraging muscle maintenance and support her to develop some mobility. I was looking at a video of us in the pool and every time Bry splashed up to Em and hugged her in the water, I would push him away. My son was coming to Em to be loving, and I was worried he might pull her down, so I was trying to protect her. Watching that video now makes me feel so sad and ashamed of myself that I am crying as I write this; I was blind to how I was hurting and rejecting him as I acted that way.

We are never going to do things perfectly, my friend. We can only do the best we can in the moment, with the best intentions. And I can't promise we will always feel pride when we gauge our actions. I feel so ashamed that I pushed my sweet, innocent, loving son away, now. I don't see a single admirable thing about me when I watch that clip, yet in the moment, I thought I was doing the right thing.

What should you do when you see your flaws? Admit them, apologise to your child, think about what you did wrong and plan how you can do it better next time the situation arises. Above all, show your child love and (perhaps hardest of all) forgive yourself. I'm still working on that last one; it is easier for me to plan the action than to take the self-loving approach. If that is true for you, too, let's agree to just keep trying to be gentle with ourselves.

It's 2021, Bry is fourteen and Emma is nine years old. Often, when I am about to lie down beside Em to say her morning prayers, Bry dives into the space to block me from kissing her and covers her face with his own kisses instead. When I go to her other side, he blocks my access with his hand. Sometimes I laugh and sometimes I get irritated. I see several things in the action. I see that he wants to give his sister love and get her love for himself. I also see his desire to be included; I think he doesn't want me to kiss Em and give attention to Em because he wants to be a part of the loving time together, and it reminds me of how he lost our attention in one fell swoop eight years ago.

I see shades of perception of unequal love, jealousy (though he loves Em dearly) and loneliness in that behaviour, and it squeezes my heart. I try to reassure him usually, by play fighting with him to earn a space next to Em, and then we do Em's prayer together and both claim a cheek to kiss, with me sometimes kissing Bry and Em alternately. Just like we all do, he wants to be loved and wants to be shown that love overtly.

I wonder about the emotions you observe as you watch the behaviours and interactions of your other children with you and/or their special needs sibling. Do you allow them to feel what they feel, or do you tell them to push it down, hide it away? Do you allow yourself to feel or do you hide your own emotions?

They aren't pretty, very often, but I think we need to let them out, see them, admit to them, face them in order to come to terms with them. You don't have to put them on display for others if you don't want to but, my friend, I hope you take the true measure of how you feel and allow your children to do the same for themselves and with you.

> Do you allow your other children to feel what they feel, or do you tell them to push it down, hide it away?

Modelling how to feel feelings and respond to them is important for your children's wellbeing, and for your own wellbeing, in the short and long term. I am a work in progress especially with this, but I assure you that my little steps forward in emotional awareness and honesty have made a huge difference to my wellbeing and Bry's wellbeing too.

Maximising Love and Value

What are some of the ways we can show our other children how much they matter to us? How can we make sure that we maximise the value they (and we) get from what we do together? I have some thoughts about this, borne out of my own trialled approaches with my son, my nephews, other children, and even my university students.

Let them feel loved
Figure out what makes them feel loved and let that guide your actions, so they receive the message of love that you want to send. As I recommend in the chapter about your love relationship, I believe understanding Gary Chapman's five love languages is invaluable here. Does your child want "physical touch" such as kisses and hugs to feel loved? Does he feel built up and appreciated and loved most when you give him "words of affirmation" like acknowledgement for getting ready for school on time or winning that last game of Ludo? Does he smile with a warm glow when you make him a cup of tea, because your "acts of service" show him that he is loved? Does he value the one-on-one "quality time" you give him, when it's just you and him, and you are showing him nothing else matters more to you than spending time with him? And lastly, does your child feel loved when he "receives a gift" from you? Practice by figuring out your own love language, then determine what language you need to use to show love to your child. Remember to give him love in the language *he* wants to receive, not in the love language you prefer to receive yourself.

Spend one-on-one time with them
One-on-one time is invaluable to build trust, strengthen connection, and communicate without words that our other child is treasured. It could be something as simple as a board game once a week, or an episode of some television show that you two never watch without

one another. Whatever you two like to do, it is good to make your time together a habitual thing.

Read. Reading together can help you share diverse experiences and perspectives, but more importantly, reading together establishes a bond between parent and child. Bry and I have been reading together since he was a baby. By the time he was two, he was stopping my reading to point out letters and short sight words he recognised, and soon enough we had started taking turns reading Nursery Rhyme and Read It Yourself books. The habit expanding to reading poems and making up stories and we came to love language exploration and storytelling together. It has built a bond that Bry and I both treasure, even today, ten years later.

Talk. When my brother gave me a boxed set of The Little House on the Prairie on DVD, that became the thing Bry and I shared, and it opened the door to talk about many life challenges including bullying, contributing at home, friendship, and special needs. If your child is not always willing to talk, maybe you can use movies and TV shows to open the door to conversation.

Play. Our time spent with our children does not always have to be heavy on the deep meaning. Give yourself and your child the gift of light play with no other purpose sometimes. Spending time rolling on the bed and laughing until the sheets are on the floor, playing cricket, or having a paper airplane race costs nothing but builds connection and creates memories your child (and perhaps you!) will treasure for a lifetime.

Know the stages of development

For children from birth up to age 6, the medical profession has produced charts and writings about their developmental stages. Get to know these stages and monitor your child's development against the stages. Let me stress that the focus is much less about putting pressure on your child to beat the clock or compete against any other child.

SUPPORTING YOUR OTHER CHILDREN

Instead, if you know the current developmental stage of your child, you can establish an understanding of the skills your child would currently be developing and design or find activities to aid skill development in fun, no-pressure ways.

I'll give you an example. When Bryan started trying to read books to me, instead of allowing me to read bedtime stories to him, we knew that he was at a stage where it was time to teach him some reading skills. We wanted him to start recognising shapes and symbols, including letters, so we covered our driveway with large symbols (hearts, squares, circles, triangles, and a few capital letters) drawn with sidewalk chalk. We wanted to strengthen his knowledge of colours while we played, so the symbols were each written in a different colour (pink, green, blue, yellow, purple, and orange). Then we drew a start line and set up a race to see who could jump on the "green heart" first, or the "pink A" first. Obviously, we held back and ran around aimlessly, pretending we couldn't find the shape for a while. Eventually, Bry learned to spot them, and his little legs would speed to the correct combo, never choosing the "orange B" if we were racing to the "blue B". In a single activity, we were having fun and managing stress, getting physical activity, developing reading skills, learning some healthy attitudes about competition and cooperation; we were showing him that we would make one-on-one time for him and growing his relationship with dad and mom. A well-designed activity can be fun and efficient all at once.

As our children begin maturing, the tracking of development remains important. Knowing their syllabus, building relationships with teachers, reviewing schoolwork done at the end of each day or week, supervising homework, and getting to know their friends are all important. Let me stress that physical wellbeing is also important, so you should be sure you are managing their nutrition and medical care, their sleep duration and quality, their dental and eye health, their physical activity levels and growth rates. For me, a lot of the heavier discussions flowed more easily when done while we were having fun. Finger-painting or playing board games or cards sometimes opened the door to shared confidences once Bryan felt really connected and relaxed with me.

Plus, knowing our child's preferences and routines can really boost connection. I found that Bry became more relaxed when he had just showered, and so he became chatty with his dad outside the bathroom door while he showered and with me when we were reading bedtime stories.

Know their preferred learning style(s)

Beyond developmental stages and syllabuses, another recommendation I have is to help your child get to know his preferred learning style(s). A good way to do that is to complete a VARK quiz[2]. This will tell which combination of Visual, Auditory, Read/Write, and Kinaesthetic approaches appeals best to your child in a learning/assessment setting. When you figure out your child's VARK style(s) (and hopefully your own), then you can begin working with your child to adapt what his teacher presents so it takes on a format that is more palatable and easily absorbed and retained by him. I do this with my University students, and they say it make studying more effective and enjoyable for them.

I'll give you some clarity by referring to the example I gave about teaching Bryan early reading skills above. When I was in school, I was taught to read by being asked to endlessly repeat my ABCs until the alphabet stuck in my head. I was asked to sit in a desk and chorus with the class statements like "A is for apple, B is for ball, C is for cat…". This approach would work well for some children (arguably **read/**

---

2   You can try an online quiz like the one at https://www.potsdam.edu/sites/default/files/The-VARK-Questionnaire.pdf, https://vark-learn.com/the-vark-questionnaire/, or any other one available free online to learn what your learning style(s) is (are). For younger children who may not be able to answer questions themselves, you would use your observations of the child to choose the most likely answers and come up with likely preferred learning styles for them.

write learners or even **visual** learners who could have enjoyed seeing the colourful letters and pictures on a chart on the wall). However, for some other children (such as children with a **kinaesthetic** learning style who fidgeted constantly because they longed to move but were told to sit quietly), that approach might not have worked so well. Drawing the letters on the driveway let Bryan run and jump and squeal and laugh so he thought learning his letters was a fun game. When we did get inside the house and open a book, he would rush to point out every A and B and C on the page, because his finger was doing the same task his legs had been doing on the driveway! For **auditory** learners we might pretend the B sound was a rumbling "b" sound in the belly of a "b" or sing a "B" song like "The Wheels on the Bus" and connect the child to the learning that way.

Adapting approaches can **become** very freeing as you begin to devise your own ways to help your child interact with materials and learn. You will be building skills in him for a lifetime of learning.

Teach responsibility and accountability

This is a heavy bit, but I think it is critical. In order to help our children develop into upstanding adults, we must groom them to take responsibility for certain things and to be accountable for doing those things. What small or (as they get older and more competent) big duties would you delegate to your child? These tasks would take certain minutiae off your own task list, while allowing your child to feel pride in holding responsibility for some of the things that keep your household running. When they are younger, these might include feeding pets, watering plants, putting out garbage bags, helping with elements of care for their special needs sibling, and even managing family finances in a small way like accompanying us to the grocery store. As they get older, more responsibility might come in helping with errands, doing repairs or gardening, doing laundry, or helping with food preparation.

Allow room for mistakes

Even as we do those things to help our child become a caring and contributing person in our world, it is just as important to teach him to be gentle with himself. I have not done this part very well, because until quite recently I was modelling the opposite. I held myself to exacting standards, I could list more of my flaws than everyone else around, and my distinct perfectionist streak led me to judge myself harshly and beat myself up mentally every day. That tendency helped me do every task at work very well, but it also had me constantly feeling anxious about whatever I set out to do and afraid that I would let people down.

I hope that, like me, you want to help your child feel a little less anxiety and a little more freedom and joy in life. If so, it becomes important to inculcate these as values and to establish behaviours to support those values. The best way to do it would be to model it and to involve your child in practicing self-care.

Let me give you an example of a time I did not get it right. Bryan was little (maybe three years old), and I had grown up in a culture that taught "spare the rod and spoil the child". Bry did some little drawing on the wall with a pencil, and I took him to the wall, showed him the marks and lightly tapped his hand and said in a stern voice, "Naughty Bryan!" Well, the next day, Bryan took me to a wall and showed me a mark he had made, then dutifully held out one hand and screwed up his little face as he yelled, "Naughty Bryan!" and slapped his own hand resoundingly. That was the most significant lesson I ever learned as a parent. I had taken my innocent child and hurt him in a way that could not be seen. He had learned to judge himself harshly and it broke my heart.

Modelling to your child that you don't take yourself over-seriously shows your child he can let his own walls down and show up imperfectly too. I love to sing at the top of my lungs and dance without caring that I don't look particularly well-coordinated. It usually gets

Emma screeching with laughter (I dance around while holding her for short periods) and Bryan joins in with me. Sean usually just looks at me and shakes his head, bemused, but there have been rare occasions when we've gotten him dancing or clowning around too!

> Modelling to your child that you don't take yourself over-seriously shows your child he can let his own walls down.

One way to shift to gentleness is to enable growth and change for our children by observing their behaviours with us, others and themselves, and then having discussions with them (when they are open) to help them reflect on their thoughts, emotions and behaviours. I encourage you to also be gentle with yourself as you try out various approaches. I can't say I get it right all the time, but I have come a long way because I've become more willing to try new approaches.

Investing Resources in Our Other Children

We've already figured out we really have to manage ourselves well to get the most benefit from the time we spend on everything we do, including our time with our other children. But time isn't the only resource that can feel limited or limiting, is it? What resources are foremost in your mind as you read that question? Are you thinking finances? Or maybe it is your own energy, or even equipment or space.

Whatever the resource that feels tight or scarce, that feeling of scarcity can really be scary or can drop your mood into the doldrums, can't it? We certainly have to shift into a new gear to learn to manage our resources when we have a special needs child. One thing that filled my head was the thought that I had to give up all my dreams of giving my son opportunities to travel to amazing places and immerse himself in diverse cultures. I had to shift my intention to save for his college education because our savings had been decimated in the time it took to get through Emma's twenty-minute ordeal.

But today, as I write this, a different message enters my mind: I have the ability to reframe how I look at the resources available to my other child. Here's my transformed viewpoint; take from it whatever appeals to you, my friend.

First, why is it that I feel Bryan has lost the ability to have experiences and grow as a person through exposure to different cultures? As a child, I did not grow up travelling around the world with my family, and I emerged just fine. Bryan may have opportunities to explore and travel later on as he becomes more mature. More importantly, he is having a whole different life experience right now: he is being a special needs sibling and it is developing him into a caring and sensitive and supportive brother, son and world citizen. The journey he is undertaking is the one within, sparked by this life experience we are having with Emma. Would I have chosen it if it were a choice on a travel brochure next to a tour of Europe? Maybe not, but this is our journey and so we are going to make the best of it together.

Second, as an educator and a woman descended from East Indian indentured labourers, I am very cognisant of how education helped my family to advance. Thus, I have held the perception that I lost the chance to save for Bryan's university education since most of what we have will need to be carefully directed toward the routine costs of Emma's medical, surgical, therapeutic, and daily care. I have held a vision that has been negative and dim for years. But isn't it amazing that we have been able to find ways to provide all that Em has needed to date? And so, I feel that it is time to shift into trusting that opportunities and resources will be available when we need them to continue to care for Em, to see to her future needs, even after we pass on. On top of that, I am trusting that all will come together to give Bryan the educational and other growth and experience opportunities that he needs to live a joyful and fulfilling life.

Does that sound a bit too optimistic and irresponsible to you, me saying that I trust that the resources will appear when we need them to support both Em and Bry? Well, I'm not just imagining a cosmic magic wand. I am shifting gears and building support systems that I have begun developing this year. This book and some message-sharing speaking engagements are parts of the system, and I'm developing training and coaching products to help people step into joy and fulfilment and leave overwhelm in the dust. I am trusting that these activities, along with my full-time job, will help me make the shift I want to see in my finances. I believe that the work I put in, coupled with genuine care for the people I want to serve, will set the foundation to keep us provided for into the long term. I value it; I am willing to envision it and work toward it.

I dare to believe that developing this system will allow me to provide the equipment and the space and the assistance that I will need to keep things working for my family. Furthermore, I believe that my calling extends to using these same systems to support special needs parents and their children with retreats and training and inclusion and advice in ways that I may not have imagined yet.

What can you lean into that will enable you to create the supportive environment you envision for your other children? What resource needs do you envision, and how can you make shifts to make them available for your children? It may not be in the same way we once envisioned but given how important our other children are to us, we have the best motivation to make it happen. Believe you can, think through the steps (i.e. how), and then take consistent action. You can do it.

Your Checklist

This chapter has shared some suggestions to help with focusing on supporting your other children in addition to your special needs child. The main ideas which were given with regard to caring for our other children are listed below.

✓ Be empathetic.
- ☐ Remember your other child is still a child, not a little adult, no matter how responsible he is.
- ☐ Put yourself in his shoes and understand what he must be feeling.
- ☐ Be gentle with him.
- ☐ Be gentle with yourself, because you are modelling for him.

✓ Maximise the love you give your other child.
- ☐ Figure out your child's love language so you can show love more as he wishes to see it.
- ☐ Make time for him, one-on-one.
- ☐ Create and explore ways to build connection.
- ☐ Build trust so you can talk with your child about his life challenges.
- ☐ Engage in simple, joyful play.

- ✓ Support his development.
  - ☐ Keep learning about, tracking, and supporting developmental stages.
  - ☐ Understand his preferred learning styles and help him learn better as a result.
  - ☐ Keep trying your hand at adapting learning approaches; your child will learn best when learning feels more like play and less like work.
  - ☐ Give him responsibilities at home.

- ✓ Reframe your ideas about scarcity.
  - ☐ Instead of thinking about opportunities lost, take stock of new experiences and growth opportunities that your child is having because of your challenges.
  - ☐ Where finances or other resources are limited, begin implementing plans to provide access to new resource pools that can benefit your family.
  - ☐ Dare to dream a bigger dream for yourself and your family. Be audacious!

I can't close this chapter without taking the message right back to our other children. You see, almost every time I look at the sibling of a special needs child, I see something magnificent. Our other children did not just develop that magnificence; I believe they were born with it: a rich vein of resilience that shores us up when we are flagging, an honesty, vulnerability, and generosity unmatched by most other children, and a maturity that far outstrips their years. They are modelling a better way for us all to live. We have the responsibility to support, love, and encourage them as their parents, but they are watching us and guiding us with their clear-eyed wisdom and pure, true love for us and for their special needs siblings.

Even as we see what amazing carers they are, we must remember that, despite their maturity and all the glowing characteristics we see in them, our other children are still children, and we are still the adults. We must give them love and attention often as well. They are amazing partners with us on this journey. We are not alone. We are blessed to have them, but we must also parent them with consistent care, respect, and love.

CHAPTER 8

Bolstering Your Love Relationship

WHATEVER RELATIONSHIPS YOU have, they are under a good deal of strain when you have a special needs child. Upon Emma's brain injury, I saw every single relationship morph immediately into a different thing altogether. A funny magic happened where I could see the band-aids holding together the relationships that remained, but people outside the relationships seemed oblivious that there was anything off at all. Do you have bandages that are holding relationships together in the way marionette joints might be held together? Have any relationships just—poof!—disappeared like a flame snuffed out, and appeared as though they had never existed? A lot of those happened for Sean and me. And the magic also worked the other way, making a few golden relationships appear out of thin air, or making one weak relationship suddenly become as strong as titanium.

In this chapter, I want to look at one particular relationship: your love relationship. I do not claim any right to make pronouncements about the rightness of your relationship. Many different love relationships exist in our communities and I expect readers of this book will have relationships that are just as diverse and interesting. What I do want to share is insight into some of the experiences and realisations that I've had as my own love relationship was impacted in our journey with Em.

If you are single, there are segments in this chapter that could be useful. I've been told by my friend who works with singles looking for love that she helps them do self-work in order to help them find a partner worthy of their love. Also, reading the rest might give some tips that you'd find useful if you meet someone who catches your interest.

Breakdown of the Relationship

Perhaps the first thing I reflected upon about love relationships when a special needs child was involved was whether divorce became more likely. The question arose because I was meeting so many single parents with children in the clinics.

For the USA, I've heard statistics that 50% of all marriages have been found to end in divorce, and I've also come across newspaper articles that reported divorce rates of couples with special needs children are even higher. Some people say this is the truth of the situation because of all the added strain and demands placed on the family unit and relationship.

I can't comment on the validity of this statistic, but I can shed light using my own experiences. In the last eight years, as a special needs parent attending countless clinics, medical appointments, therapy sessions, conferences and training sessions as well as doing volunteer work with other special needs parents, I have interacted with at least a few hundred other special needs parents. I estimate that half of those I interacted with shared that they were single as their love relationships had ended. Not all told me whether the break was exacerbated by the special needs situation, but several did.

There were various times at which the breakdown of their relationships happened. A few moms told me the separation was an immediate walkout when the child was diagnosed as having special needs or when the child was born with unforeseen special needs. In most cases, though, it appeared to happen after months of trying to function in the new paradigm. It sure made sense to me: even caring for a non-disabled child is stressful and leaches energy and time away from a romantic relationship, so the stress can become super-sized when a child has special needs. Not only are parents trying to cope with the demands of parenting, but they are also trying to figure out the extra needs of their special child. There is no "Carers' Guide to Special Children" textbook to tell them what the formulas or hacks are, because each of our children is located in a unique place on a very broad continuum, and has different challenges, abilities, and needs.

> Caring for a non-disabled child is stressful and leaches energy and time away from a romantic relationship.

Let me explain why I wanted to write this particular chapter. It is not about "blaming" our special needs children for relationship decline. It is about facing up to the fact that there are added challenges that special needs parents must cope with and trying to provide a little extra support to people with whom I empathise.

Busy, busy, busy

I imagine that, much as Sean and I experienced it, romantic partners begin passing one another like two ships in the night, doing all the busy work and taking any spare moment to finally squeeze in the opportunity to brush our teeth or shower at 2 o'clock in the afternoon or morning. One is waking through the night and handing over responsibilities to the other at the crack of dawn, only to shift, bleary-eyed, into our full-time jobs or other aspects of life.

I've been waved off with this discussion before with a statement like, "Well, every parent has to wake through the night with a sick child; we all get by." That used to make me feel terribly sad and uncared for as well as roaringly angry because what everyone forgets is that special needs parents are likely to get just a couple of hours of sleep each night *for years*. That's what they do to prisoners of war: sleep deprivation is one of the most dreadful ways to torture people.

The other thing we've been told is, "Well, just take turns sleeping!". I wish it was so simple, but when you're "off duty" with your special child, you still have cleaning, cooking, and caring for other children (or God forbid, doing overwhelming costume-making homework assigned to your other child by an overenthusiastic teacher!), your full-time or part-time job, shopping for food, going to appointments, researching interventions or doctors, finding equipment to support emerging issues, and…well, you get the picture. That does not cover what happens when someone in the house or extended family gets sick or a visitor shows up without calling first. Plus, far too often, when you do go to sleep, you can hear your child crying or vomiting and you know the pain your significant other (SO) is enduring through those small morning hours. How well can you sleep anyway?

As you can see, the circumstances can easily grow the distance between partners, while influencing the pressure in the relationship to build. If there is not time for basic self-care, then there is less time for a date or physical intimacy, even for an intimate conversation. And that does not even take into consideration the mental aspect of being free enough of mind to be able to laugh and be light, or to carry a deep conversation.

With nobody available with whom we can discuss what we are going through (because it is hard for other people to understand if they have not been in our shoes), even the smallest conversation easily turns into an argument because frayed nerves and lack of sleep just predispose us to having quick fuses and misunderstanding one another. I know the solution is to go "talk with someone" like a counsellor or a psychologist. To do that, we must budget two scarce resources: time and money, and also feel guilty about speaking ill about our SO, who we know is doing their absolute best. So, after Emma's injury, I never made it to the point where I could talk with someone like that, and neither did Sean. I do think that as we learn to shift our priorities and time, and free up some funds, some counselling could be of use, so that remains on my list for future action.

Here is my secret. I have never told this to my closest family, so if they ever read this book, they will find out here. Sean and I had great big disagreements and spoke about divorce many times before Em came along. I endured a lot of pressure and abuse in several of my past jobs and the stress would spill over into how I interacted with my husband during those first thirteen years of marriage. Sean tried to be there for me, but I bottled it up and if it came out, it was venom-like and often directed at him. Otherwise, it led me to hide away behind the safety of a book or sleep, and so there was growing distance between us. My own communication skills left something to be desired, especially back then. When I did want to discuss difficult things about our relationship, that didn't work either because Sean's style is to be quiet and mine is to talk (and yell) it out. He would never want to risk saying something wrong, and I would never want to risk leaving anything out, in order to clear the air. So, our talks would inevitably end in frustration on both sides and eventual silence and distance.

When Em became brain-injured, I started to read to find out what we needed to know about causes, recovery, interventions, and more. I started to ask more questions including trying to learn about the experiences of other people who had dealt with brain injuries from the ICU. Sean retreated inside himself, and I felt scared that he was broken. He focused on Emma's every need, and Bryan's too. We put on an act for Bryan's sake; Bryan was 5, and we would pretend to laugh and feel joy with him right there in the ICU next to Em's bed, although we were so terrified and in pain every minute. I expected the situation to magnify our issues and lead almost inevitably to divorce.

I look back now and I realise that we are still together a further eight years on, because we both decided we would do whatever it took to see to both our children. Our united focus defined our values and cemented our marriage through all the ups and downs following Em's brain injury. But those shared values were all about sacrificing our own well-being and happiness to take care of our children, and we did not allocate any time (nor did we see the need to prioritise allocating time) to invest care for one another.

I don't know you anymore

Little wonder that, one day earlier this year, while talking with Sean about my thoughts about spirituality and Emma, he seemed surprised to hear some of what I was saying. It had been many years since we had spoken of this sort of thing, and we had been walking through a spiritually challenging period, so we had evolved in many ways, including our perceptions and beliefs related to religion and spirituality. We did not have time to finish the conversation that day, but it was the longest and most earnest talk we'd had in years and Sean reluctantly ended it saying he'd never thought of things that way and there was much to consider. For me, the realisation was that our individual beliefs have likely evolved in almost every area, and there are few that we've stayed abreast of with one another.

Can you see how easy it would be to pause one day, look at your SO, and wonder who that person is that you're sharing a life and family with? To suddenly find yourself saying, "I don't know you anymore"? For me that is one concern, and the other is scarier to me: that one might end up thinking or saying, "I don't like you anymore," or worse,

"I can't share this life with you anymore". This, I know, happens in love relationships in general, but I do feel that coping with special needs situations does exacerbate the challenges.

The Way Forward

Honestly, the idea of waking up and no longer liking my SO terrifies me. I think I would feel abandoned, and also scared if my marriage ends because I have implicitly trusted Sean for over twenty-one years of marriage. And that is not even considering how hard it would be to parent a teen and a special needs child if we are apart from one another. So, this is the map I've structured for you and me to plan our way forward, my friend.

Know yourself
The first step must be loving yourself, realising or remembering that you are amazing just as you are. I've spent some time in recent years just getting to know once again who I am, what I think, what I want from my life, and what my dreams are. As my picture of myself got clearer, I felt the hole in the centre of my chest start to fill in because I was starting to realise I was enough, and I did not need someone else's approval for me to feel worthy.

That evolution brought me to a place where I began to realise that both Sean and I deserve happiness and fulfilment in our relationship as well. And so, I have begun to set aside some time to get to know what I want in, and from, our relationship. If you are like me, you may have powered down your aspirations for your relationship, but based on my newfound clarity, let me tell you, you deserve to be loved, and to give love, my friend. Invest a little time to

> *You deserve to be loved, and to give love.*

love yourself enough that you plan for your relationship to thrive and grow and feed you, and for you to give genuine love and care to your precious SO.

Relationship resuscitation

It would be wise to also have a chat with your SO and get him/her to give thought to the same thing. Now depending on the kind of person your SO is, this may be easier said than done. Maybe you can't tell them or ask them to do such a thing. Maybe they will sneer or bark at you or brush off the idea. Here is an approach I use in such a situation.

I don't tell someone with resistance, "I want you to do X". Instead, I chat a bit and just mention, "You know, I've been doing something different recently…" and then share about the importance of knowing myself and what I want from a relationship. I confide that I'm spending time getting clear on what I love, what I would like to do differently to give more and get more in my relationship, because that relationship is so valued, and I want it to thrive and last. Do you see how sharing in that way would not be so threatening to your SO, but instead just drops some breadcrumbs?

Well hopefully, your SO will ask you to share what you've been thinking. You can truthfully say you've only just started thinking about it, but you'd love to hear their thoughts on it as well, because their opinion is so important to you, too. That opens the door for you to invite your SO to do some introspection and dreaming about your relationship and how you two could strengthen it together. Do you see how you could word the request rather like you care enough to plan to resuscitate your relationship together instead of casting blame?

Then make a date for you two to sit and share your thoughts in order to come up with a shared vision for your relationship. Ideally, that vision would include a shared part and a part where you both get to be individuals. This is because the more in tune you are with yourself, and the better you can fulfil a bit of what you feel called to do as an individual, the more joyful and fulfilled you will be, and this spills over into how you act with and toward your SO. Don't forget to discuss what you want, and what your SO wants, as an individual; think about how you two could carve out time and other resources to support that for you both. Normally, when your SO sees you leaning into making his/her individual calling a reality, the joint relationship plan would receive more focused and joyful energy.

One point of resistance is the issue of time. We have discussed how there is never enough time even for sleeping and self-care, so I am very aware that finding time to rebuild or invest in your relationship with yourself would be very difficult. If we want our relationship to last, if we want to feel true partnership with our SO, if we want to be together to model a loving relationship and to give support to our children then we will eke out the time for this as well. Since part of this required me-time, I began to find that in between-task increments of just a few minutes at a time. I found I could connect these mini me-sessions to simulate a longer think session by journaling my thoughts so each idea from an incremental session was captured and could later be strung together with others like beads on a chain.

First steps

Let's talk about this relationship plan a bit. I'd suggest a couple of things: brainstorming ways to show love, making arrangements for competent childcare so your mind is not on your child when you two are together, and routinely scheduling uninterrupted time together, including finding your way back to meaningful physical intimacy.

There is an idea of five love languages put forward by Gary Chapman (I mentioned this briefly when speaking of caring for our other children in the previous chapter as well). He says people feel loved when you show them love in one of five ways, and it is

Find your way back to meaningful physical intimacy.

important to give love to them in the way that matters to them, *not* in the way that matches your love language and therefore matters most to you. To put it simply, if your SO only speaks English, it would be a waste of energy to say I love you in French: "Je t'aime". And if you speak only French, you'd need to hear French words, because English would seem like gibberish to you. Using Gary Chapman's advice, if you and your SO speak different love languages, you two could each begin showing love in ways that would be appreciated by the other. As a specific example, someone might feel most loved when she receives a physical gift, while her SO might feel loved when he receives a massage from her (an act of love).

I will admit to a massive level of discomfort when I think about leaving Emma in someone else's care. With the exception of one aunt a few years ago, Sean and I have never had family care for Emma; most people seem so nervous even holding her for more than a few minutes. The few times we have had no choice but to leave Em alone while the two of us go off together, we've found ourselves talking about her and Bryan. We wondered if they were okay, and then gave up our time together by texting or calling to check. You do need to find a way to get care for your child beyond the two of you. Maybe you can train and lean on family members, church friends, volunteer groups, and so on, or you could (as we do) hire a nurse or (if facilities exist in your country) access carers through governmental or NGO disabilities support programmes.

Talking about our relationship revealed so much to me but the biggest news might sound familiar to many people. We both wanted different things from our relationship. More specifically, we placed different things as our top priorities. For me, it was spending time together so we could work on our friendship, as that would nourish the love once more. For Sean, it was finding more time for physical intimacy. We both got irritated at each other because we couldn't appreciate each other's perspective. It took a while for us to be able to respect one another enough to open hearts and minds enough to listen, but we eventually accepted one another's opinions. This takes considerable effort to do, but I hope you decide the effort is worth it.

Now here is the bit that feels forced in the beginning: scheduling time together. There will never be time, unless you schedule a trusted carer to come spend the evening. There will never be money unless you recognise a special date as an investment in the long-term wellbeing and survival of your family. You will never be in the mood for physical intimacy unless you remind yourself of the wonderful characteristics of your SO. Notice all the generous things they do for you and your children and be generous in turn. Stop being distracted by all the other things you have on your to-do list and schedule time together. Oh, and don't underestimate the importance of variety. Even if you schedule a date once a month to start, add some variety: go out or sit down at home to dinner as a couple, take a walk together, watch a movie, have a picnic with the kids and ask your carer to come along to help with your special needs child.

I need to add one little thing to the relationship resuscitation plan. It is tiny but it is also the most important thing of all, to my mind. Do you remember when your relationship was in its early days? Do you remember any of the following:

- how excited you felt to be around your SO?
- how you couldn't wait to see them again?
- how special their voice was?
- how kind you were to them?
- how much you laughed together?
- how their corny jokes were endearing and not something that made you roll your eyes?
- always finding a way to give them a little present or a kiss or hug or smile or nudge?

- being eager to share the details of the day: something nonsensical that made you laugh at work, or some success you had?
- sending texts, jokes, photos, reminders, or questions to them a few times a day?
- holding hands or giving a peck when you were leaving for work each day and when you got back home?

In my case, when I walked into the house, Sean would have a hot cup of tea waiting for me when I came home from work. It told me he loved me every single evening without a single word. Do you see how the little things kept you warmed up to one another, connected in both heart and mind? Figure out how to sprinkle a few special little things back into your daily lives. A word of caution: if you do none right now, start slowly with one or two things and slowly increase. Too many too fast could be irritating or overwhelming for one or both of you.

Planning for the longer term

As your short-term resuscitation plan comes to fruition, you get to celebrate it. I encourage you to actually talk about your progress as a couple. When companies undertake a big project, they have a project manager, and they track progress against the plan. Well, resuscitating your relationship is an important project for you two. While you don't need charts and typed reports, you should review progress and discuss challenges and whether to try new strategies or continue using those that are working well.

With all the communication and connection gains you all could achieve in the resuscitation project; you'd be well-positioned to trick out your relationship even further. Just like you would have worked to share your dreams and wants in the short term, have another series of discussions to paint the picture of where you want to grow your relationship to in another five or ten years. Is there a goal you both share as individuals? Maybe you want to partner up to work on that together and it could bring you closer. Some of the content of other chapters could come in handy, but the important thing is your hand-in-hand approach to achieving the vision you will build together.

Your Checklist

The journey of a special needs parent is a lonely one in many ways, and your significant other may be the one who walks the path closest to yours. Here are some of the main action ideas that might support you as you empower yourself to build or rebuild your love relationship.

✓ Recognise the stress you're facing and how it can affect your love relationship.

✓ Consider whether professional help can support you in strengthening your relationship.

✓ Reconnect with yourself.
  ☐ Who are you and what do you want now?
  ☐ How have your beliefs shifted?
  ☐ Accept and embrace your individuality.

✓ Get to know one another again.
  ☐ Talk more openly and more often.
  ☐ Reconnect to the fun and the joy you used to feel with one another.
  ☐ Know each other's love languages, so you can show love in the language they can best receive.
  ☐ Recognise your shared values.
  ☐ Recognise and accept your differences.
  ☐ Leave room for both of you as individuals even as you build yourselves as a couple.

- ☐ Establish and work toward a shared vision.
- ☐ Regularly schedule time together to do what matters to both of you.
- ☐ Build variety into your dates to keep novelty in the relationship.
- ☐ Shift gently and slowly into a newer way of thinking and behaving; it's more likely to stick if changes are slow and steady.

- ✓ View your efforts to build or improve your love relationship as a project.
  - ☐ Know your short-term focus.
  - ☐ Know your long-term focus.
  - ☐ Squeeze a little time for your relationship resuscitation into everything else on your schedule.
  - ☐ Review progress by discussing success and challenges and adapting approaches as you go along.

So much of your plan or approach will vary compared to any other couple. What you do and how you do it will be customised to fit who you are. Despite the uniqueness, my dream for you is a strong sense of self-worth both in you and in your SO, a mutual connection and love for one another, and the security and happiness that comes with that.

CHAPTER 9

Boosting Your Health

I ADMIT, BEFORE EM was hurt, I was very lax about self-care. When we suddenly became special needs parents, there was even less opportunity for it. Time became so scarce that many days it was 2 p.m. before I got a chance to brush my teeth, I had not slept even an hour during the night, and I'd been walking with Emma before the crack of dawn at 5 a.m.

Have you been unable to make time to attend to your own well-being? As special needs parents, our beloved children often take the lion's share of our time, energy, and attention. That leaves us feeling scarcity of time which consequently means we're not giving sufficient care to ourselves.

Do you feel a longing or need to create better life balance and see to your mental, spiritual, and emotional wellness? This idea includes eating healthily and on time, getting enough sleep, engaging in intentional movement/exercise, and maybe even fitting in a social life. I intend to share the positive and negative aspects of our own experiences along with the practices we have relied on. I am far from perfect in this regard, but I have been making sustainable changes little by little, and so I hope that the next few pages give you some ideas and encouragement.

No Time to See to Your Health

A frequent complaint I have encountered when talking with special needs parents about their health is not lack of awareness, but a conviction that they can't find the time to invest in their own health. I attribute a similar thought process to why my own health (and Sean's health) steadily declined during the period 2012 to 2019. By 2019, I was in my mid-forties and feeling like I was already heading downhill on my life rollercoaster. My weight had ballooned, my organ function lab tests had been flagged, I was pre-diabetic and experiencing extreme joint and back pain daily, and I had a high heart-risk rating.

The real incentive to change came in mid-2019, when Sahara dust blowing across my country caused me to rely on a nebuliser multiple times a day for about 30 days to cope with a spate of asthma attacks. I genuinely felt like I was at death's door. I was terrified because my family depended on me to be there. If I died, Sean would be all alone, not only physically caring for Em, but also financially providing for her and Bryan. Worse, what would be the situation if we both passed on?

> Time invested in my own health is an investment in my family's survival and well-being.

Finally, I understood that revitalising and then maintaining my health was not going to be selfish in the least; time invested in my own health is an investment in my family's survival and well-being.

Spot Your Health Red Flags

I've already shared about how ignoring my own self-care caused my health to deteriorate, but it would be worthwhile to outline some of the major physical, mental, and emotional consequences you might need to pay attention to.

Physical pain. This can be one of the most overwhelming things you experience. Not only would pain prevent you from doing daily tasks, but it can prevent you from even enjoying any parts of your day. Some of the big ways in which I've heard special needs parents speak of experiencing pain are: headaches (related to stress, tension and lack of sleep), back pain (especially neck pain indicating tension and stress and lower back pain due to stress or lifting our children or being overweight), joint pain (perhaps coming up due to extra weight or inadequate nutrition, or as a symptom of arthritis), and stomach/belly pain (such as from indigestion or even Irritable Bowel Syndrome that may come up with long term stress).

In the case of chronic back pain, it might start most days as soon as you try to get out of bed, might prevent you from straightening up for several minutes or more before you can walk around more normally. Sometimes, just turning in the bed could be extremely painful. You might experience stabbing or pulsing pains in your lower back or zapping down your legs, from lifting your child and carrying them around repeatedly. I know this kind of pain can be terrifying because you would worry about reductions in your mobility, physical ability to care for your child, and the degree of support you can give to your significant other with the heavy work.

Stress-induced weight gain or weight loss, and declining confidence. You may have read books that explained that when we are stressed, our body increases production of the stress-hormone cortisol. In turn that makes our body hold on to weight. I think of it this way: if our body feels stress, it concludes that we are likely to have a life-threatening circumstance soon, so it tries to hold on to resources to protect us. We may hold on to extra weight, storing up calories that we may need to keep us alive in our time of impending starvation or disease. That could explain some of what is causing you to gain any unwanted weight.

Some other special needs parents have said to me that when they look in the mirror, the person who looks back at them looks like a stranger, with droopy jowls and a fat face and body, and others have told me they just lost too much weight and see only skin and bones. Due to their eroding self-confidence, many have really stopped looking at themselves in the mirror. That behaviour was true for me too. Plus, when I was overweight, I became embarrassed to interact with others and open myself up to scathing remarks that some people would mete out to me.

If you are concerned about whether your weight is healthy, an easy first step you can try to include is checking your Body Mass Index (BMI) to tell you if your body weight is above, below, or at the normal range for your height and age. The BMI is a good rapid indicator for most people, but very muscular people like body builders may find that their extra muscle mass incorrectly gets them assessed as "obese". Another useful check is to do a body composition check on a home, pharmacy or gym scale, as it assesses your body fat % and body muscle % as compared to average for your age and height. This helps you decide whether you want to increase or decrease your weight and how healthy your body composition is at the time of evaluation.

Declining lab test results and illness. Many of us special needs parents are so swamped by all the demands on our time that we don't prepare healthy food. If you just grab a sandwich or have a cup of tea and some biscuits like I commonly used to do, then most of your nutrition consists of carbohydrates and sugars. Eating convenience foods reduces your intake of fruit and vegetables and increases your consumption of processed foods that are full of salt, sugar, and unhealthy fats, as well as preservatives, colourings, and other chemicals. If you don't consciously make better food choices, your body will not be getting enough variety and quality of nutrition.

A lab workup would give you a breakdown of your health markers so you can spot and reverse any areas that are out of bounds. This reversal does mean that you may be able to find your way back from chronic lifestyle diseases over time, as well as bounce back from short term signs and symptoms. Perhaps this is obvious, but it bears stating: a doctor would be the best person to request the lab tests for you and meet with you to interpret the results.

Low energy and mood. You would likely be seeing declines in your energy and mood due to reduced sleep and all of the stress you have to bear. Your body needs good nutrition to promote good physical and hormone balance and help you manage energy slumps and mental and emotional swings.

Establishing Habits

Other than getting enough sleep, there are four things I recommend you should fine tune to get the inputs you need for better health: your diet, intentional movement, breathing, and (though it may seem a stretch) addressing the way you think.

Diet

Friend, when I speak of our diet, I do not mean to convey the idea of dieting. That is a very different thing. Most people use "diet" to indicate a short-term way of eating that causes rapid weight loss, often followed by rebounding weight and disappointment, either because the diet was unsustainable or because the body does not reach an equilibrium weight and returns to its accustomed higher weight. Instead, when I speak of our diet, I mean to convey the ideal human way of eating.

Have you ever thought about why you eat the way you do? Do you recognise certain patterns in how and what you choose to eat? When I paused and took a conscious look at my eating, I was very surprised by what I found. My eating habits were not at all desirable. I could see more clearly how my whys were skewed and had been depleting my energy and eroding my health.

I found that my eating was done mindlessly for the most part. I did not only eat when I was hungry. I ate by the clock: breakfast at breakfast time, lunch at lunch time, and dinner at dinner time even when I was not hungry. That in itself may not be so much of a problem, but on top of that I ate many empty foods as snacks in between. These snacks served as fillers, not for my stomach, but for my emotions. When I was sad or bored or frustrated or lonely or scared or feeling trapped in the situation with Em, I looked for crunchy cookies or chips. The snap and crunch gave me emotional satisfaction and release, even as I filled up on empty calories. I hope you make better choices than I did, but if you see yourself reflected in my behaviours, let me reassure you that all is not lost. You have the opportunity to bring about sustainable change for your and your family's health.

The first big idea to ingrain in your thinking is that not all calories are equal. It is not a matter of just keeping calorie counts low as you may have heard in some diet programs. This is because you can consume fewer calories, but if you do not choose nutrition-rich foods, you will not provide your body with the building blocks for a long, healthy life. For example, if you eat potato chips, what would you get nutrition-wise? Near empty calories, mostly starch that the body converts to simple sugars that flood your bloodstream and make the body keep craving more as it hunts for the nutrients it needs.

In addition, our way of eating (especially in Western cultures) has evolved over the last century to include many processed foods that cannot be considered natural in the least.

If we want to overhaul our health, the best place to begin is with reflective questions. Why do you eat at the times you do? Why do you choose the foods you do? How good are your food choices for you? What triggers you to eat when and as you do?

The best news I have is that I began releasing weight and experiencing improvements in energy, pain levels, and even incidents of asthma, within the very first month of making changes to the way

I ate. (Note: I'm just going to structure the information in a very straightforward and concise way to be less overwhelming and more relatable to you. This may sound a little like a lecture because of the lists to come, but I genuinely care about giving as much information as I can to you. After that, it will be up to you to choose whether any of my recommendations appeal to you, and to then make long-term dietary shifts that suit you and your family). Please remember that adopting positive eating habits will always help you to improve your health, and you don't have to do it all at once. Small shifts made over time can make a huge cumulative positive impact for you.

Water Intake

There is so much to be said about water intake, but here are the basics. Our body works better when we consume more water because our body is over 60% water. We need fluids to help our brain, heart, lungs and muscles (all over 70% water) work effectively, our blood to shuttle carbon dioxide and oxygen and nutrition to and from our cells, our digestive juices to break down our food and extract nutrients, our lymph fluid to support our immune system, and our excretory system to eliminate waste products from our bodies. The best hydration we can get comes from plain water and adults should drink at least eight glasses (a minimum of 2 L) of water each day. If you drink coffee, tea, or other products with caffeine, know that these dehydrate you and so you should drink an extra cup of water for every cup of these products you consume.

Sugar and Sugar Substitutes

Sugar is perhaps the single most detrimental food to our wellbeing. Our pancreas secretes a hormone, insulin, into our bloodstream to help us process sugar to derive energy and clear excess from our system. However, if we are constantly consuming sugar either knowingly or unknowingly (as it is hidden in many foods), then our blood tends to contain a high amount of sugar throughout the day, every day. As a result, our pancreas must keep making and secreting insulin to keep dealing with all that blood sugar. Over time, our body's ability to respond to the insulin and purge sugar becomes less effective, causing us to become insulin resistant. Then, more than before, our body tends to take excess sugar and, instead of purging it out of the body, store it by converting the energy to fat. This fat affects how we look and feel and how well our body works. I have two specific concerns about us storing so much fat. First, it traps toxins that may leach into our body, instead of being purged efficiently. Second, higher fat levels have been linked to higher risk of Type 2 diabetes, heart disease, stroke, and high blood pressure. Little wonder these are the most common lifestyle diseases, right?

The first big positive dietary change we can make for our own health is to remove as much processed sugar from our diet as we can. We will still get plenty of natural sugar from fruits and vegetables, but I highly recommend cutting out sodas and other drinks that are sweetened and reading labels to spot sugar (sugar hides in our food under dozens of names). Science is showing that people who use artificial sweeteners have an increased chance of obesity and diabetes, so don't be fooled into thinking that sugar substitutes might be a better choice, either.

White/Refined carbohydrates

Our body easily converts white carbohydrates (wheat and other grain flours and products like bread, roti, rice, pasta, and even white potatoes) from starch to simple sugars and these sugars flood our body and create a sugar high. As explained in the section about sugar above, an over-consumption of these foods can really pump up our body's production of insulin and lead to insulin resistance and increased fat storage, for example around the waist. There are better carbohydrates that you can put on your plate. These include complex carbohydrates like ground provisions (sweet potato, yam, dasheen, cassava, etc.), plantains and green (cooking) bananas, breadfruit and other gourds, and starchy vegetables such as carrots and pumpkins.

Processed Food

Until 2019, most of my diet was processed food. I ate sausages often, plenty of canned foods and bagged foods, and foods in boxes. The big WOW came for me when I started to read, not just skim, the labels in the grocery store, and really think about what I was choosing to consume. When I started to read the ingredient lists, I found that my food was not really sounding like food at all. There were natural and artificial colourings, sweetening agents with names that were virtually unrecognisable as sweeteners, stabilising agents, preservatives like mould inhibitors and colour and taste enhancers, and unhealthy oils galore. Newsflash: NONE of these are good for us!

I also found some foods that purported to be good for us that were terrible for us. For example, I switched to almond butter from using peanut butter because peanuts are likely to carry aflatoxin from mould. One day Sean did the grocery shopping and a new almond butter brand got into my home. It tasted of nothing, just empty and quite bland, and that made me read its ingredient list. A big element in there was that the almond butter included palm oil. Why would palm oil be added to almond butter? I suspect as a cheap filler to bring down the cost of producing the food and make more volume of the product for a lower price. That leads me to share with you about the quality of our fats.

Fats and Oils

I used to have the idea that fat was yucky and not good for me at all, but that is absolutely untrue. However, it is important that we choose to consume good fats and not bad fats. Let me explain.

We actually should be seeking to eat healthy fats to provide our body with the fatty acids it needs to function optimally. I learned that there are unsaturated fats and saturated (also called hydrogenated) fats, and we need to avoid saturated fats as much as possible because their long chemical chains are hard for the body to purge, and because they are high in omega sixes, which we get too much of. Instead, we should be seeking to consume more omega-3s and these come from many seeds (e.g., chia seeds, flaxseeds) and nuts (e.g., walnuts, macadamias, brazil nuts) as well as oily fish (e.g., wild salmon, sardine, mackerel, tuna) and avocados. In terms of good oils, I've heard that olive oil, grapeseed oil, coconut oil, and avocado oil are among the best to use. If heating them, only use low heat to reduce hydrogenation. Heat will string molecules together into long chains of carbon and hydrogen and oxygen that are hard for our body to process, use, or purge, and therefore hydrogenated fats are unhealthy. For similar reasons, when buying oil, look for cold-pressed oil.

You may have heard that in the 1960s, flawed advice was given to us that fat (not sugar) was bad for us and linked to heart disease. Well now, we are learning that the opposite is true, and we should avoid processed sugar and sugar substitutes and actually seek to include some good fats in our diet.

Milk and milk-containing products

I wonder if, like me, you grew up having one or two glasses of milk every day? No matter their financial hardships, my mother and father made sure we had a warm cup of milk every morning and night to strengthen our bones, nails, and teeth. I should also mention that I have been asthmatic all my life.

My journey into seeing milk differently began with Em's brain injury when the respiratory technician advised that many children who are bedridden die of fluid build-up in their lungs and suggested that maybe we should look for an alternative to milk. We switched Em to almond milk within a matter of months and she has never had any fluid build-up challenges, thank God.

However, it took me over six more years to apply this knowledge to the rest of my family. Only when I had 30 days of asthma attacks in June/July 2019 was I forced to ask myself what I could do differently. I did some reading about research into the effects of milk on the body and found some things that concerned me: claims of milk-sourced calcium being difficult for the body to absorb, while calcium from plant sources like celery (isn't it amazing how celery looks like a long-bone?) is very easy for the body to use. I also heard claims that Scandinavian populations which consume more milk per capita also have the highest bone break statistics, so that made me pause and consider whether milk could actually be less good for my body than I had been taught.

I loved my bread and butter and bread and cheese sandwiches a couple of times a week, I had multiple cups of black tea with milk every day, and once or twice a month, I would have a bowlful of milk with cereal as a late-night snack. I woke up every morning with a phlegmy throat, and stuffy sinuses. And my asthma was even more of a problem due to increasing intensity and frequency of attacks. Out of desperation, I stopped milk and milk products, and within a month I realised I had stopped even having phlegminess. Every one of my challenging respiratory symptoms had disappeared.

So maybe stopping the use of milk and milk products is something you'd like to try out for yourself. At the very least, I strongly endorse it for your special needs child.

Fruits and Vegetables, including leafy greens and bitter greens

We already know fruits and vegetables are great for us, right? But in my home, I focused on foods that were convenient, and that meant we did not have near enough reliance on plant-based nutrition. You might ask how come sugar is not good for us, but we can eat fruits. That's because fruits are high in sugar as well as water and fibre. All the extra water dilutes the sugar making its way into our body, and all the fibre requires us to work harder to process the food as we digest it, releasing energy more slowly into our bloodstream. Plus, fruit is not only delivering sugar and starch to us. It also contains many micronutrients that are important for the strength and proper functioning of our body. For example, citrus fruits are critical to strengthen our bones and prevent rickets, and celery contains calcium and magnesium that are valuable for our bone health and prevention of muscle cramps.

All vegetables are important, but the absolute best would be leafy greens, including bitter greens, such as kale, spinach, amaranth (dasheen leaves), dandelion greens, arugula, broccoli, collard greens, pak choy and bok choy. I consider bitter gourd and okra when I list bitter greens in my mind. All veggies and fruits, but especially leafy greens, are packed with phytochemicals (micronutrients) like various good salts, antioxidants, and vitamins that boost our health.

Plus, remember that the more you cook plants, the more you break down (reduce) their nutritional value. Thus eating raw salads, fruits, green juices, nuts, seeds, and sprouts are some powerful ways to pump up your immune system.

Meats and Fish

If you are vegetarian or vegan, be careful about getting balanced nutrition, because there are a few nutrients readily found only in meat. If you don't eat meat, you should get supplements to round out your nutrition.

If you do eat fish, then make sure you include plenty of oily fish in your diet, to provide you with omega-3 fatty acids. The best oily fish would be tuna, salmon, sardines, and mackerel, preferably wild caught as the nutrient levels are higher.

And if you eat meat, grass fed, organic offerings are recommended. As a rule, choose lean meat, and if your meat is cured, then watch out for extra sugar and nitrates/nitrites which have been found to increase your risk of developing cancer.

Intentional movement

Intentional movement is critical for your wellbeing. In terms of walking, you are recommended to move at least 10,000 steps per day in order to not have risks related to being sedentary. But walking is not the only choice available to you. Choose the mode of movement that appeals to you. You might do yoga, weightlifting, running, biking, skipping, swimming, or even trampoline-jumping. What counts is having fun and keeping your body active. You may find it useful to three aspects of body health: your strength, your flexibility and your endurance or stamina. When you choose your activities, you can research ways to work on each of the aspects. It is generally recommended to build up strength first and then work on the others.

Breathing

Have you ever noticed how you breathe when you are stressed? Your breathing gets shallow and rapid, and you feel your stress level climbing. Well, when you breathe deeper, slower breaths, that sends a message to your nervous system that everything is safe in your surroundings and your whole body relaxes. That drops cortisol production, and your stress level drops drastically. I think you'd be providing better oxygenation to your blood as well, since deeper breaths fill up your lungs (not just the tops of your lungs).

You can significantly boost your health just by taking the time to breathe slowly and deeply all the way into the bottom of your lungs for 5-10 minutes two or three times every day. Then, when you breathe out, empty your lungs as completely as you can. A simple 4-4-4 breathing pattern works well for me (4 counts as I breathe in fully through my nose, 4 counts as I hold the breath in my lungs, and 4 counts as I exhale all the way out of my mouth). You can research and try out various breathing exercises and choose whichever deep-breathing routine feels good to you.

Positive thinking

I would be remiss if I left out positive thinking as a big influencer of wellness. Practicing gratitude shifts your happiness level upward and removes a lot of the stress you will feel every single day because you begin training yourself to not have a negativity bias. Gratitude does not suddenly convert you into a person who giggles endlessly, but it does make you happier and prevent you from living in a mode where you expect things to go wrong almost as a default. I encourage you to read up about our brain's negativity bias and the power of shifting it[3].

In addition, the practice of being present has been a life-changer for me. This does not mean you forget about the concerns regarding your child's health or the many things you are juggling. Nor does it mean that you stop planning for the future or working to put things in place in a strategic way. It just means that you are able to reduce how much you worry about things that you cannot control and do the best you can for your child, your family, and yourself by focusing on and enjoying whatever you are doing in the moment.

---

3 This is an online article explaining the psychology concept called "negativity bias" and explaining its implications as well as how we can shift it.
https://positivepsychology.com/3-steps-negativity-bias/

Your Checklist

I hope the following list can help you sort through the ideas presented so you can decide your priorities to make any adjustments that you think could help you and your family boost your health and longevity.

✓ Assess your current state of health and wellness.
- ☐ What elements are you feeling the pull to improve?
- ☐ How do you look and feel?
- ☐ What is your energy level like?
- ☐ What are your body composition and BMI statistics?
- ☐ When you work with your doctor, what do your lab tests reveal about your blood sugar and other blood workups, cholesterol, heart risk, other organ functions (like liver, kidneys, and thyroid), and other health risks?

✓ Take a critical look at how you eat.
- ☐ When and how often do you eat?
- ☐ What triggers your eating? Are you eating for nutrition or to fill an emotional void, or for some other reason?
- ☐ What foods (high nutrition content) do you gravitate to?
- ☐ What non-foods (low nutrition content) do you gravitate to?

- ✓ Give yourself better nutritional value.
  - ☐ Drink at least eight glasses (2L) of water each day.
  - ☐ Reduce or remove sugar from your diet as much as possible.
  - ☐ Reduce or remove white carbohydrates as much as possible and rely on low glycaemic index carbs instead.
  - ☐ Cut out processed foods.
  - ☐ Choose good quality fats and oils.
  - ☐ Replace dairy and dairy products as much as possible.
  - ☐ Consume a largely plant-based diet, with fruit and vegetables and plenty of bitter greens.
  - ☐ Try to consume a good portion of your fruits and vegetables in uncooked or minimally cooked form to their nutritional value high.
  - ☐ If you eat fish and meat, choose oily fish and lean meats.
  - ☐ If you don't eat fish and meat, research what supplements you need to provide balanced nutrition.

- ✓ Get the right input for your body beyond just diet.
  - ☐ Practice intentional movement for strength, flexibility and endurance.
  - ☐ Breathe deep and slow.
  - ☐ Practice positive thinking and mindfulness.

CHAPTER 10

Improving Your Financial Situation

BECOMING A PARENT brings financial responsibilities, I know you know that. I bet those financial responsibilities increased past your expectations when you began the journey with a special needs child. If only our love was enough, right? Maybe, like me, you've thought that. But providing financial resources is a part of the way in which we fulfil our duty to our children, and it is also an expression of our love for them.

In this chapter, I want to talk about some of these things, not the way a financial planner or accountant or lawyer would, but in the way it makes sense to me as a parent who wants to put things in place for her children. These are the big issues I think about, so these are the ones I will share with you in this chapter:

> *Providing financial resources is a part of the way we fulfil our duty to our children.*

- earning enough income to live on
- planning for emergencies
- financial instruments/planning for your child's support even after you pass on
- how to provide for your other children's needs
- planning for your retirement
- daring to hope for more than just a life of subsistence.

Earning Income and Saving

The first financial decision that had to be made after we came back home with Em was to figure out if there was some way to care for Em while maintaining my job and my earning ability. I absolutely had to keep earning if we were to continue covering the expenses incurred in just the first few weeks as we made a round of assessment visits to doctors and therapists. Another financial shock was the receipt, months later in the mail, of a bill amounting to between two and three years of my income for the services that had been provided to us after the incident that caused her brain damage. Over the years, many unexpected matters came up: illnesses and needs for scans and x-rays and specialist visits and upgrades to equipment to support Em's rapidly growing body. Psychological care also emerged as an issue and that came with a significant price tag as well.

I believe that the first place to start is day-to-day *expenses*. What are the elements that you must be able to afford each month? Groceries/food, medicines, nurse/caregiver, medical and therapy visits, utilities, travel to work, insurance, other payments that are due. List them out and write out the costs for each element. Next, write out your monthly *income*. How much income does your household earn after tax? Will your income be enough to cover your non-negotiable expenses for the

IMPROVING YOUR FINANCIAL SITUATION

month? If not, then you must reduce your expenses and/or increase your income.

Saving or reducing spending is possible by doing things like trading services or trading products to cut down on expenses. Some of the things Sean and I have done include sharing produce from our backyard with neighbours and friends, and we also receive produce from them. In the case of a wonderful woman[4] who does developmental therapy for Emma, we have satisfied her expectations that we work with Em well enough on our own that she does appointments with us once a month instead of twice per week. That saves us both financially and timewise (we live far away from her office). Similarly, with Em's beloved speech therapist[5], without insurance support, we are having to carefully balance the frequency of visits so that we can control our costs.

For a few years, we could not buy too many gifts so we would sometimes give gifts that we or the children had received. Other times, I made handmade gifts or baked items to serve as gifts. For us, entertainment bills immediately went to zero because we didn't have the time to go to a movie anymore, nor was there financial padding enough to go to a movie or to dinner had we wanted to.

We also made big reductions in our expenses by finding alternative places to buy from, not buying things we considered unnecessary, downgrading some services to basic plans. I put some of my teaching sessions back-to-back. It drained me energetically but saved me about six hours of commute time each week reducing my fuel and car maintenance spending as well. We've established a backyard garden and herb garden, and that has reduced the cost of buying market vegetables. We do most of our food preparation at home, and this boosts

---

4 Carey Phillipps, Director of Edutherapy Ltd.
http://www.edutherapycaribbean.com/team/carey-phillipps/
5 Lysca Welcome-Tenia, Director of Lysten To Me Speech Therapy

our control of the quality of food we eat, thus enhancing our health while reducing what we would spend on buying pre-cooked food.

In all of that talk about saving, I must also mention that sometimes I seek to save our time or protect our health as opposed to our money. Every year I take my son to low-cost concerts at Christmas time, because I want to just share a joyful experience with him. I also splurge on tickets to a single pricier, professionally produced Christmas concert, and if his cousins want to come along, we feel even happier to feel the love of family as we laugh and sing and dance in our seats. Later on, as pressures took a toll on my son and on us, we added some counselling to our list of must-haves. Sometimes we had to "save" on a week of one activity to afford some other activity. I think almost every special needs parent understands how to juggle appointments in order to manage financial outlays.

Boosting income has also helped, though finding time to put into a side hustle is tough with a full-time job and special needs child on the roster. I have picked up a few coaching and speaking opportunities to earn some extra income as I follow my entrepreneurial dream. I've also been developing and rolling out training programs online, while Sean dreams of hydroponics yields that create a thriving income stream.

Planning for Emergencies

The routine expenses are one thing, but I am sure you sometimes lie awake at night trying to figure out how to set enough aside to cover for emergencies. Sean and I have insurance, and that insurance has covered some of Em's expenses. However, therapy and several other claims have come back denied, and we've never been able to find out why we are not being covered. I'll be honest: I'm so darned tired working for Em and my family, that another fight for insurance is beyond me at the moment. Therefore, I have been prepared to work harder, create side jobs to earn more to save for emergencies, in order to avoid the frustrating non-answers that we get when we begin pushing for resolution on some things, like insurance queries.

I've heard the recommendation that you should build up an emergency fund to 3-6 months of expenses. This makes sense for regular situations. Beyond this, consider whether your child has any conditions that could make emergency care necessary. If you live somewhere that you know you can walk into an emergency/urgent care department and receive immediate and free attention, I am so happy for you because you won't have to carry a larger emergency savings amount. However, if you don't have access to free and prompt emergency care and feel that you would likely need to pay for it, then consider further building up the value of your emergency fund.

There are some other things you could do to support you in an emergency. Explore whether you can set up an insurance plan with critical injury/disability riders that would give you a pay-out if certain health events occur with your child. In some countries, like mine, the existence of what the insurer would call a "pre-existing condition" would likely prevent such coverage, but legislations and guidelines differ from country to country, so check it out for your state/country.

Planning for After You Pass On

A top-level worry for us is what would happen to Em, especially, if we pass before she does. It's a hard thing to write, but it is the ugly truth. If we are so stretched caring for her, even with our love and our duty, it pains me to speculate on who might be willing, and who might be able, and who might be loving and self-sacrificing enough to take on this massive responsibility for a child who is not their own. All those intangibles are one thing, and we must add the financial element on top of it: this is huge! Who would be willing to sacrifice their

> Who would be willing to sacrifice their financial comfort, the resources they have for their own children, their own retirement, their personal development or recreation, in service of your child's support?

financial comfort, the resources they have for their own children, their own retirement, their personal development or recreation, in service of your child's support? And if there is nobody willing or able (or trusted by you), then would your child go into a private home or into state care?

If no finances are provided by you, the direction is going to be state care. If you have made arrangements financially, then some more protection and control can be put in place. If we were to die tomorrow, we would not be in a place financially to put Em into a protected space; I would be praying with my least breath for her safety and heart-centred care, knowing that I had not put things into place for her in the long term.

Specifically, there are two things that we are working toward to change where we stand: a will and a trust.

Will

I know you must have heard of people leaving behind their "last will and testament". Your will sets out what you instruct to be done with your property and earnings once you pass on. Your will also sets out your wishes about what you want to happen regarding the care of your children, if they are legally minors or disabled dependents, instead of having the courts decide. Having the will witnessed and registered through an estate attorney is highly recommended to make it an official document. Until the will is fully actioned, there must be someone who controls and manages the resources. Having a will helps things to transition more smoothly and reduces the likelihood of family squabbles or involvement of the state to make decisions about your estate.

Long before you write anyone's name into a will as your children's stipulated guardian, you should have discussed the task to make clear what "the job" would entail and to get their agreement. Certainly, it would be wise for you to assess their fitness for the role, including their ability to bring up your child in a way you'd approve of. Maybe you'd also want to give them the chance to feel out the role by spending some time babysitting, either with or without you present.

In the case where you leave your property to children who will inherit it when they reach a certain age, this resource manager would be important to perform duties such as distributing stipulated amounts to a caregiver or guardian of the children for payment of expenses like groceries, schooling, clothing, medical, therapy, and other needs. Emergent needs and growing needs would also need to be catered for, such as if surgery needs to happen, or a new size of wheelchair must be sourced and purchased, or laws change and mandate new actions to be taken or services secured to support your child's care.

Trust

I found out that a trust is a second instrument that could provide security for our children if we pass on. It especially feels like a useful tool as it can help retain more of what you earn to be allocated for your special needs child's care, by reducing how much is "lost" in paying taxes. If you set up a trust, you will be moving your property into a situation where your property is owned by the trust, and income earned can be paid out for use in the care of your child. You also need to shape the will in a special way to ensure that whatever resources you want to be vested in the trust do end up there, even if you've omitted the attribution of some of them before you die. Having a trust allows a trustee to oversee financial disbursements from the trust such as control of issuing of funds to a guardian who must spend your funds on your dependent children.

Trusts cost much more than wills to put into place, and they are more complex to administer and to update, because as life circumstances change, the trust terms need to be amended to stay up to date. However, trusts bring added levels of security and retain more finances for use by heirs, and therefore they may be particularly useful to those of us with special needs children. Thus, consider working with an attorney to find out details about what type of trust would be best for your needs, and how to structure it.

Providing for Other Children

I feel like having a special needs child tends to take up a majority of our time and energy. Because of this, I honestly still feel guilty about how my family life shifted from being so supportive and connected with Bryan to 90% focused on Emma after the brain injury, instead of a much more even split as I had intended.

I noted that financial support gets distributed to things that are urgent a lot of the time, and our special children's needs often fall into the "urgent" category. On the other hand, our other children's needs seem less pressing and so they get relegated to the "when I have it" or "not until I have to" category of things we'd like to do. We know our other children's needs are important, and they deserve some mindful planning, so here are some things you might want to consider.

Our other children need preventive care, and they also might get sick from time to time. If you don't have a health insurance plan that covers your entire family, check out what options are open to you. It could cover dental and eyesight check-ups, other treatments, and support you with a large percent off or percent repaid to you if you need to access the care of a doctor or surgeon for your other children.

This would be more affordable when you get them through a group health plan at work.

I know how stressed I have always felt regarding savings since Em's surgery and brain injury. A big chunk of our savings got wiped out just managing the surgical bill, and for several years after that, we were using much of what we had to pay off the bills related to rehab and therapy. Right now, Sean and my full-time jobs handle our monthly expenses but there is nothing going into savings. I am concerned about that because savings are necessary to help us set aside for retirement and for emergencies.

Worst case scenario, when we pass on, if there is no nest egg to cover remaining expenses, and to provide for the care of our children, I would be heartbroken. I do not want to ask someone to care for them and bear all the expenses as well. For that reason, right on the heels of Em's brain injury, Sean and I took out life insurance coverage on both of us. Whichever of us dies first, the other will receive a pay-out to support the family's expenses moving forward for at least a few years. And when the second of us dies, that pay-out will be able to support the financial upkeep of our children, through the trust that we hope to set up.

One thing that I cried about after Em was hurt was the loss of my ability to save toward a University education for my son. I felt that the education hopes I had for Bryan were forced into second place because Em's survival and recovery trumped all else. Someone lectured him at age 7, "Bryan, now that Emma is brain-damaged, you have to win a university scholarship to help your mom and dad!" and that really pushed my buttons. How dared they?! I know the pressure Bry is under each day in our home with helping with Em's care, and I refuse to add a demand for a scholarship to everything else that is on his shoulders. I told him all we want is for him to do his best. I prefer a sane and happy son to a stressed out, possibly anxious or depressive one who wins a scholarship just to get mom to leave him alone.

Finally, over eight years after Em's brain injury, I am mentally in a space where I can start thinking about wanting to support Bryan as well. Unless there is a life and death kind of emergency, we do not spend what we do not first receive in our hand, so we operate by spiriting away payments to health insurance and life insurance. We have also begun stashing away a little every now and then toward Bryan's tertiary education. We still have four years, and any little bit is going to help, we remind ourselves.

Planning for Retirement

I hope that in the midst of all the rest of the financial worries, you are daring to hope for more than just a life of subsistence. This year the dream of being able to do more for and with myself after retirement has begun to flare into life. How can we do that?

Well, I'll tell you. I totally wished for more income but even though I had ideas, I acknowledged to myself that I did not have time. To find time, I had to sacrifice something, and I started sacrificing sleep even more. Sean and I would sleep two to three hours at most each night, and I felt so stressed. That, however, was what was required to do our jobs, supervise Bry's homework, and care for Em day and night along with all the other day-to-day tasks of home life.

One day, a close family member came over and she had such a look of distaste on her face as she spoke to me, that it cut deep. She said, "Couldn't you at least make your front yard look presentable? Can't you even grow a hedge?" and she wiped her finger through a layer of dust on a side table and sneered. I felt hurt, and I also felt very angry. Standing up for myself made me rude to her, and I attacked with cynicism, telling her I chose to care for Emma instead of my front yard.

The truth is that we have to sacrifice something to get by, given our life circumstances. That experience made the point clear to me. I was sacrificing my mental and physical health worrying about doing everything, and I was still woefully lacking based on the judgment of so many people. That was the day I started to face the fact that my own judgment is the only one that should matter to me, and from that flowed some peace and freedom. My home became even messier as I asked myself what I wanted from life. In the last year, I began painstakingly taking back time to build the elements of that life for my family's wellbeing in the long term.

The biggest thing that we need is supplementary income. There is no savings on our current income, and that means we needed to create side gigs for ourselves. Sean has stepped in even more to support Em, which has allowed me to start building my business around writing, coaching, training, and speaking. I strongly believe that where attention goes, results grow.

I mentioned life and health insurance earlier, and that is also important to support yourself in retirement. I think something else you should explore is a certain kind of insurance coverage that are referred to as "critical care" insurance, which would support you in case you need treatments for stroke, heart, cancer and the like, all of which become more likely as we get older. Don't forget your best health insurance is taking care of your health now, my friend, and there are many tips in the chapter on health.

Research investment options as well, as you seek to provide for the future. If you are close to retirement, be sure to get advice specific to people who can afford to make high-risk investments.

Where attention goes, results grow.

Your Child's Purpose and Legacy

Often, people think of legacy as entirely financial. My idea of legacy was shaped when my father died, because so many people came up to me in the decade following his death to speak about how he impacted them and shaped their values and the way they live. Therefore, I think of legacy as how I will live on.

I see Emma's joy and positivity despite her challenges, and I can't help but ascribe some higher meaning to her being here. I believe she is effecting change in the world, starting with her impact on our family. And now, because of the evolution of the way we perceive things and how our attitudes, hopes, plans, and behaviours have shifted, I feel that she will be leaving a rich legacy herself. For example, this book is a part of Emma's legacy.

Is your child speaking to you, whether or not they can actually verbalise a thing? What do you see as your child's purpose? As an example to stimulate your thinking, you can ask yourself if your child, through their journey, are doing any of the following:

- Tightening connections within your family or network of friends.
- Raising the standard of care because of the advocacy you engage in with them.
- Bringing awareness to a cause or a situation.
- Growing networks of people dealing with a particular condition.
- Teaching doctors to shift their views or evaluations of special needs persons in a particular situation.
- Improving access to caregiver support.
- Improving access to information.
- Improving access to funding.

- Boosting resilience of special needs parents and families.
- Enhancing support given to special needs siblings.
- Opening up possibilities for insurance for special needs children.
- Creating a platform for our special needs children to be seen, heard, and respected.
- Building acceptance and awareness so our special needs children no longer belong to an invisible population.

The list of potential purposes for our children is unending. Just open yourself to the possibility that you can tune in and know what it might be, and over time, I pray the knowledge will filter into you, as it is doing from Em to us.

Conclusion

This chapter may have been a hard one to work through. Finances are challenging. Such varied emotions come up: self-judgment, shame, hope, anger, worry, pain, fear, joy, ambition, pride, concern. If you skipped over some tough parts, that's perfectly fine. You don't have to do them all at once, and nobody gets to tell you what to feel or do.

I do encourage you to take a bit at a time and let yourself face it all and feel it all, because as we feel it, we get to mentally deal with it. We can purge some of the negative emotions and limiting beliefs tied to childhood experiences and heal. Then we can begin to visualise and start building a better financial situation for ourselves and our family, and even more people beyond that. That is what I wish for you and your family, my friend. I am daring to wish it and build it with my family in the same way that I am encouraging you to do.

Your Checklist

The insights from this chapter can be summed up as follows:

✓ Earning enough to live on.
- ☐ If special needs medical, therapeutic and other care are significant additional expenses, how will you earn enough?
- ☐ What day-to-day expenses/spending can you reduce and which are non-negotiable?
- ☐ Can your current income cover your non-negotiable expenses? If not, then you need to further reduce expenses/spending or supplement your income.
- ☐ Reduce expenses by trading services/products, giving handmade gifts or re-gifting, cutting out entertainment expenses, shopping at less expensive places, downgrading to basic plans, lengthening some work days to reduce commute costs on other days, and growing some of your own produce.
- ☐ Sometimes, as hard as it may be to do this, you may have to adjust which therapies and equipment you access, and when/how often. Working with your therapist, you may be able to do some of the interventions at home, with the therapist checking in less frequently to provide oversight.
- ☐ What choice are you making: full-time at home with your child, part-time at a job and part-time at home, full-time at a job, or creating side gigs in

addition to a full-time job? No answer is wrong; find what is right for your family.
- ☐ There is no shame in honest labour. Better to try and fail and try again than to give up without trying. Get clear on your dream and work to make it real!

✓ Planning for emergencies.
- ☐ Build up a routine emergency fund of 3-6 months of expenses.
- ☐ If your child has conditions that could make costly emergency care necessary, over time you should seek to build your emergency fund up further by this amount.
- ☐ Look into insurance plans with critical injury and disability riders that could provide some financial help if your special needs child or others in your family have an emergency.

✓ Planning for your child after you pass on.
- ☐ As a priority, get a witnessed and registered **will** prepared to instruct on what happens to your property and earnings when you pass on.
- ☐ Clearly identify in the will who will perform roles such as managing assets and caring for your children.
- ☐ Consider if a trust will serve your needs, as it can reduce taxes and routinely disburse funds to care for your children.

- ✓ Providing for your other children's needs.
  - ☐ Plan to get important tasks done, and not only focus on urgent tasks.
  - ☐ Consider insurance plans to see to preventive health care and other treatments for your whole family.
  - ☐ Check into life insurance, which may provide a pay-out to care for your children if you pass away with limited savings.
  - ☐ If saving for a university education or other long-term goal is important, then whenever you can, stash away a little a few times a year. Any little bit helps.

- ✓ Not forgetting your retirement plan.
  - ☐ Dare to hope for more than a life of just subsistence.
  - ☐ Life does not get flat and empty after retirement. You can start another career or ramp up your side gig into a full-time business.
  - ☐ Start your side-gig now; you don't need to wait for retirement to start.
  - ☐ Don't let naysayers dampen your hope and drive; your judgment is the one that matters. Your dream for yourself and your family is what counts so make the sacrifice.
  - ☐ Your special needs child's legacy may fit into the work you do as you structure your retirement plans.
  - ☐ Get advice and do research about what investments you could participate in to provide for the future as well.

CHAPTER 11

Celebrating Your Resilience

I BELIEVE EVERY SINGLE one of us who has special needs children already had what it took when we were taking the first step of the journey as special needs parents. However, I know it wasn't easy, not then, and not now. I feel empathy for you, and I feel it because as I look back at the Marcia I was eight years ago and the Sean my husband was then, I feel such a pull on my heartstrings. I want to cry for you all and for us, for the innocence we lost, for the pain our special needs babies have endured, for the attention our other children have not gotten, for the financial cares we couldn't even imagine before this particular chapter in our lives, for the guilt and the doubt and the worrying, for the careworn brain that never stops relentlessly thinking, rationalising, hoping and praying for things to work out, for a miracle.

I don't expect us all to have the same beliefs or perceptions, so there will be parts that you may agree with, other parts you may vehemently disagree with, and some parts in between. I have shared my views as openly and fully as I can (within the limits of memory, cognition and emotional wherewithal) with the wish that my experience might help you achieve clarity and support as you walk your own path.

Your Challenges Make You

I used to feel that the big challenges in my life were breaking me. All I saw was how unfair and harsh the world was. In truth, life as it is now still has some hefty challenges that hurt and test me hugely, but my ability to grow from challenges has shifted considerably.

I have never enjoyed my big life challenges. I have sometimes prayed to God asking for them to be taken away, and I have even prayed to God at various low points in my life, asking Him to not make me wake up the next morning. Life challenges are painful! What has made special needs parenting the most painful experience of my life has been seeing my child become hurt and knowing that it is not an "owie" I can kiss and make better. One day, I will not be here, and she will face the world alone, and I must do all I can to help her develop without any guarantee that she will be able to do so. Without knowing what she will need for this future, I must provide for her financially, physically, emotionally, and more.

Shortly after Em was brain injured, I spoke with a cousin who shrugged off what had happened. He said to me that we all have a purpose in life, and apparently, I had been born to give service to my daughter. I read into his two sentences that I should just buckle down and accept my fate. I felt resentment, and I felt alone. Where was the comforting and the commiseration, the gentle hug of a loved one? The fact was it was not there, but what was there was a message I was resisting at the time: my life circumstance was not going to change so I'd better align my thinking and feeling and actions accordingly if I wanted to be less traumatised every single day for the rest of my life.

We don't have to understand everything or make everything feel smooth and perfect in our life; how rough and unpretty my authentic life is right now, but how much joy and fulfilment it also gives me!

My friend, the whole point of this section of the chapter is to reach out and clasp your shoulder reassuringly. Special needs parenthood is a role that closes up your throat and squeezes your heart far too often. But every time you feel that, you are feeling it because you care for your child. You are feeling it because—with your eyes full of tears—you are daring to raise your head, stare all your old rules in the eye, and insist you *will* persevere. You ARE persevering. Not only for your child, not only for the rest of your family. For *you*. You are doing this because *you* count. This situation has not broken you, and nothing that is coming is going to break you either, as your life with your child moves on. And that is because you are resilient.

> Special needs parenthood is a role that closes up your throat and squeezes your heart far too often.

This is Your Time

You are resilient, I will say it again. You are alive because countless generations of people have survived so you could be here, so you could share the gift of who you are with the world. Adaptations from those generations have been passed on to you in your very blood through your DNA, in your learned behaviours through your culture and ingrained habits, and even in the memories and emotions and beliefs in your heart and mind.

There is also what you bring to the table, for you are not just a product of the past. You are a powerfully thinking, feeling, and intuiting individual, and your power resides in your ability to shape your reality and your perception of that reality. My dear friend, there are so many who decided that they could not cope with the weight of being a special needs parent, and I know you understand how that

> You are alive because countless generations of people have survived so you could be here.

could happen. But you did not decide you could not. You decided to commit to your child, and I know that to be so because you chose to read this book. You *have* had choices, and the choice you have made is to step into this role as a special needs parent, to struggle, adapt, love, and dare every single day. Do you recognise that only a phenomenal fighter does that?

I see you as a real-world Rocky (do you know the movie?) powering through the life challenges that threaten to break you and emerging from each with such inner strength and life lessons to bless the rest of your life. If you take a little time and jot down all the lessons that life has taught you, all the capabilities it has generated in you, all the insights you have developed, and the way you have come to let your inner voice guide you, then you begin to get an inkling of the unshakeable resilience that resides within you. Though unseen, that resilience is so very real, and sensed by those who see you. Your special needs child knows, feels, and depends on that resilience daily. Today, I want *you* to connect with that knowing and celebrate it.

Your position as a special needs parent is established and you have made it a part of your identity. No matter how heavy it may feel, it is not a curse, because you have chosen to continue fulfilling this role of special needs parent.

Though we have not met, your journey fills me with hope, because this is exactly the thing—the love, the commitment—that connected us across space and time. I do feel that I know you, that on a soul level we know each other and each other's children, because we share this aspect of our journey.

Finding More Joy

Science has discovered that humans' thoughts are twisted. We are predisposed to seeing the glass as half-empty, rather than half-full.

CELEBRATING YOUR RESILIENCE

They call it our negativity bias, and we think that way just to stay alive. The brains of ancient man evolved to keep him alive. If he was able to forage and hunt in a particular area or in a particular way and provide for himself and his family, he just kept doing that because he knew he would survive. If his patterns were not providing enough sustenance and security and safety, then he would push himself out of his comfort zone and try something new until he found what improved his circumstance, and that would become his new comfort zone. His brain was wired to quickly send him alarms about what did not work, about what dangers were on his horizon, about what could threaten his life. Therefore, a predator noticed some distance away would send everyone on alert. Human brains learned to always look at different things, unknown things, new things as threats not just to our comfort, but to our actual survival.

In today's world, very little around us threatens our survival, but our brain doesn't know that. Our sympathetic brain, also called our reptilian brain, is our alarm system that wants to keep us safe. It floods us with messages about the negatives in our world, not to complain, but to keep us safe, securely ensconced in our mental and physical caves. This boosts our negativity bias, so we can't easily perceive the glass as half full, as I mentioned before. I want to encourage you to start giving yourself a fairer picture of the world around you, so you can see more light, joy and possibility around you. It will make your circumstances feel so much better even though very little will have actually changed.

(Maybe at this point your logical brain is sending you a snarky message. Mine used to, but I shushed it up. I do not want to live in a dark and dreary version of my world. It is already challenging enough as it is; I want some light and singing and laughing and twittering birds. I hope you do too and keep reading for your own sake.)

I have three suggestions that will work alongside your natural resilience to elevate you. From being a care-worn woman with her head down and constant debilitating back pain seven years ago, I now actually catch myself smiling and laughing and singing for no reason except I am happy to be alive, happy to be surrounded by the love of my family, happy to be building a life with more possibilities than I could have imagined a year ago, and light within my heart and mind.

My three suggestions may sound trite, but they have worked wonders for me. I suggest giving them a try for a week or two and noting any difference for yourself before you make a decision to drop them.

Gratitude

Shift that negativity bias with the first practice: being grateful. You definitely have time for this, because it takes me two minutes every morning when I wake up. All you do is identify five things you are grateful for, whether big or small.

At this very moment these are my five:

1. I am *so* grateful that I actually believe I am worthy enough to be writing this book.
2. I am grateful for my loving, trusting, joyful Emma in the bed in the next room.
3. I am grateful for Bryan who just came into the room to ask for a kiss because he needed to know I would choose him over my work. (Actually, I am grateful for his mischievous laugh as he did it!).
4. I am grateful for the warm bread and cheese and cup of tea I had for breakfast. It was just the comforting start I needed to my day.
5. I am grateful for the two beautiful green, black, and white butterflies I saw in my back yard this morning. They took my thoughts to my Dad, and made my heart lift up on light wings as I watched them cavort through the air.

You get to choose everyday little things like I wrote above or bigger, weightier things. Many people choose to write their gratitude list down in a gratitude journal. I do that only sometimes; I do not beat myself up for not being more consistent with writing my list out because it is the gratitude and not the logging down that matters most. I find that I want freedom and choose not to be locked into yet another documentation routine that feels constricting and opens me up to harsh self-judgment.

If you can't come up with five gratitude items in your present, try connecting with what you are grateful for from any point in your past. I believe it is the feeling of gratitude that opens up my heart and my outlook, so I source my gratitude from my past sometimes.

Did you list your gratitude yet? If you haven't, I hope you take a minute now to draw a few deep breaths in and let gratitude actually fill you up and flow out through your gratitude list. Should you find that you don't want to stop at five, laugh at how the exercise filled up with joy so fast, and keep going! Make it a game and see how many you can get to. If you have the chance you can even play the gratitude listing game with others around you.

Affirmations

Gratitude by itself was not enough for me. Indeed, I think that if we are always smiling, it does not necessarily mean that all is well. An empty smile is not enough, because I get more from life when there is purpose behind my joy. That is why you may have noticed I mentioned "joy and fulfilment" together a few times in this book.

The second suggestion I have for you is to begin making affirmations, which are positive statements that help you to visualise and believe in the wondrous elements that are being created in your life. You must first be able to emotionally and mentally connect with a vision for your life before you can bring it into being (i.e., believe it and then be able to build it).

Some examples of affirmations include:

- I am doing my best.
- I choose to be happy and to love myself today.
- My possibilities are endless.
- I radiate confidence.
- I am in love with myself and my body.
- I can change my life and my situation.
- I am more than my negative thoughts.
- I am healthy and happy.
- I always make the best decisions for myself.
- I am enough.
- I let go of my worries and stress.
- I live in a house with a lovely garden.
- I love to exercise.

They are fairly short and clearly note what state of being is desired and they are written as if they already exist, even though they may, when stated, be only a dream or vision.

Now let me be honest with you. These traditional approaches to stating affirmations don't always work for me, because my logical mind calls me a liar when I say some that are a stretch. My inner voice says, "Marcia, you know you don't have a perfect body," and then I look down at my mom-tummy that I am hoping to slim down, and it confirms I am a liar. Or it says, "What a liar! You know you never stick to your exercise routine long enough to make it a habit!" And so, I have changed my approach to stating affirmations. I have taken my inner logical voice and converted it from the voice that calls me out to the cheerleader I need. Instead of just affirming a future desired state as though it were reality, I create action-oriented affirmations. These are affirmations that are in the present tense (as they are meant to be) but say something like "I am doing X because I know Y" or "I feel so good when I X and I am seeing the change in Y".

These are some action-oriented affirmations that I might state related to the health and fitness I want to improve for myself:

- I am fit and energetic.
- I love the way that exercising daily is helping strengthen my body to support Emma.
- I am thrilled that my lung capacity and endurance are increasing as I take on more taxing exercise programs.
- I feel so proud that I am able to do dance steps that are more intricate every day.
- I never miss my daily workouts because my brain, flexibility, and coordination are all making huge leaps forward.
- I can't wait to dribble that ball around Bryan and dunk a basket every afternoon because my aim is better, and my teenager is active and smiling and we are growing closer. It's just a matter of time before we trick his dad into joining us!

Do you see how I fit my actual current version of life into the affirmation wording? Do you see bits of my personality in there, my desire to connect with my family, to endlessly tease Sean, to hold Emma, to become more coordinated (as I love to watch dancing but can't dance very well myself)? With my reframing of my affirmations, my logical mind has no chance to call me a liar and so it has to become my supporter. This affirmation approach makes my vision more likely to become my reality because my reality is the foundation.

Now you try it, my friend.

Self-love

I grew up being told I was not good enough, or at least that is the label that I took on as my identity. I was asthmatic so I was told not to run around and to stay inside. I became less active and more sedentary, and the way I sought approval was by being a good student. The challenge was that no matter how well I did at school, I would always be told I needed to do better. If I lost a few marks, I'd be asked to explain why I'd made those mistakes. I'd feel so small and stupid that my confidence just kept shrinking. My self-esteem took a real dive, and sadly, my issues with self-confidence and self-worth continued into my working life. It took decades before I matured enough to realise I did not need external validation to be able to like myself and trust that I was good enough.

I hope you have already learned that lesson, my friend, but if you are still working to internalise that, let me say it to you. You are an amazing, resilient, loving, and adaptive person! Exactly as you are right now, you are worthy. *You* are enough! You already have it within you to face whatever comes. Whatever comes, you will always be able to adapt and grow, learn and progress, and make a difference to your special needs child and your family, and in this world. There is no need to be perfect, just be gentle with yourself and allow yourself to be unapologetically you.

Your Checklist

The last chapter celebrates your innate resilience and recaps some approaches that can enhance your resilience even more.

✓ Trust in your resilience.
- ☐ You had the resilience from the very start to support you on this journey as a special needs parent.
- ☐ The more you shift into a growth mindset the easier it becomes to face challenges and keep adapting and growing.
- ☐ Insist that you *will* persevere, no matter what comes.

✓ Why you are resilient.
- ☐ You are the product of countless generations of survivors, so you have been bred to survive and to thrive.
- ☐ You have the will and the desire to commit to your special needs child.
- ☐ You are a fighter with formidable skills and strength borne of your life challenges.

✓ How to enhance your resilience by shifting your negativity bias.
  ☐ Practice gratitude.
  ☐ Use affirmations.
  ☐ Love and accept yourself, regardless of external judgments.
  ☐ Let your child's joy and light bolster you.

Epilogue

As the book draws to a close, I want to share an acronym poem I wrote to celebrate Em's light. May we always find the light that our special needs children are shining for us.

Emma's Light on a Tuesday
This morning I woke, tired, again.
Under the covers, I heard a familiar refrain:
Emma was laughing, her voice a high squeal,
So full of life, her joy the real deal.
Do I feel joy of that magnitude, and how often, if yes?
And what reasons have I to feel any less than blessed?
Young at heart, loving circle, and possibilities untold—I filled up with gratitude and the call to laugh bold!

Appendix A

Our Foot Massage Routine to Help Emma's Constipation

NOTE: This massage routine was built from research into pressure points and reflexology. Though we do not know the many sources to acknowledge them by name, we express our gratitude for the meaningful benefits we have seen with Emma's constipation challenges. It is believed that the upside down U-shape of the massage path stimulates the colon, which is similarly shaped (and you can see that in a foot reflexology diagram). If you want to try this method, it would be wise to do your own additional research, and to consider checking with your doctor as well. We have only used enemas once or twice in the many years since we started doing this massage.

Sketch of the massage path:

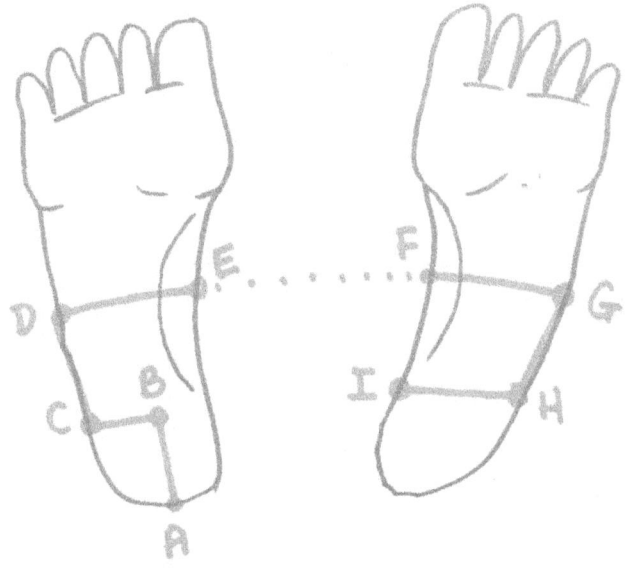

The steps we follow:

(Press gently with pad of thumb as you move through this massage from point A to point I. Each massage movement consists of a smooth glide with a steady, gentle pressure. This should feel like a relaxing, soothing massage and you should never be pressing enough to hurt.)

1. Sit directly facing the feet to be massaged. (We always remove footwear and do skin-to-skin massage using clean hands.) Always start the massage on the Right (R) foot.
2. Follow the path starting with light pressure at **point A** on the sole of the right foot and gliding your thumb up the heel to press gently into the centre of the heel at **point B** for about

5 seconds. (This is just a little precursor step that lets Em know that we are starting to do the massage.)
3. Glide your thumb to **point C** on the outer edge of the foot. (This stimulates where the small intestine meets the large intestine.)
4. Massage upward along the outer edge to **point D** about halfway up the foot. (This step is believed to stimulate the ascending colon.)
5. Glide with steady pressure horizontally across the right foot to the inner edge of the foot, i.e. to **point E**, at the outer edge of the right foot.
6. Continue the glide directly over to the inner edge of the left (L) foot, starting at **point F** and massaging over the sole to **point G** on the foot's outer edge, just about halfway down the foot. (Steps 5 and 6 are believed to stimulate the transverse colon.)
7. Glide your thumb down the outer edge of the foot until **point H**, about another quarter-way down the foot. (This step is believed to stimulate the descending colon.)
8. Massage across (this may be at a slight angle) from **point H** across to **point I** on the inner edge of the foot, which lies just where the instep meets the curve of the heel. (This step is believed to stimulate the last section of the colon.)
9. Press for 10 seconds on **point I** of the left foot with your thumb. (This relaxes the anal sphincter muscle, and often helps to ease Emma into evacuation, even when she is tensing up and fighting her body's call to pass stool.)
10. Repeat the sequence from start up to 5 times or so, and if evacuation does not happen, try again in a few hours to several hours.

Appendix B

Marcia's Five-Year Vision Statement

The following is a recent version of my five-year vision statement, updated in January 2021 as I dared to dream of a better life for myself, my family, and those I would serve through my young business.

On January 31, 2026, I stretch as I wake up to the sound of the song "This Is Me" from the soundtrack to the movie "The Greatest Showman". With a grateful smile, I spend a few minutes meditating to guide my day right. I already know my clear goals for today, and I eagerly jump out of bed into the joy that awaits. My family is sleeping and, in the quiet "me" time, I drink a glass of water and spend half an hour exercising and listening to a wonderful audiobook I have been eager to start. I feel so pumped to be growing, body and mind, in this half an hour. I take the next half an hour to make a healthy breakfast for my family, and I review my plans for the day as I eat and have my tea.

Today my online courses will continue to be taken by hundreds of students, and my team has scheduled my daily minimum of two coaching calls for me. I'm only taking a few calls today because today I'm doing a visit to the retreat centre that we have developed to help special needs children and their parents. We also offer face-to-face workshops around the world six times each year, but I always include joyful work with at-risk groups like those special needs families, because their families are reflections of my own. Later today, I will finish another draft chapter of my third book; this one is in support of my efforts to help regular people start their own businesses and thrive by aligning who they are with their Soul's purpose. Also, I have so many ideas for courses that I want to develop, and I quickly jot down those ideas before they fly away with their muse.

An hour later, my family is awake, and I run over to share kisses before Bry and Sean leave for school and work. Bry will likely be off to another country next year for University. He has grown into a compassionate, hardworking and clear-thinking young man. He is fit and smart and caring. I know he will build a good life and career for himself, but I will miss having him with us at home. I realise I will even miss his smart comebacks and millennial wit.

I hear my name being called by Emma, who is now fourteen years old. My eyes fill with tears of joy as she walks to the front door and reaches up to greet me. Just five years ago, she was in a bed and unable to speak or control her limbs. I say another silent prayer of gratitude for the miracles wrought in our lives. Emma has lived a story of big challenges and miracles and my heart swells as I connect to the awe of having watched her teach doctors the power of living in hope and love and consistent effort. We do our daily prayer and healing session around the table and share updates about what each of us has planned for today.

Across the table, I catch Sean's eye. He no longer looks so tired and broken. Now, he is fit and his skin glows. He is still a teacher; it is his calling, and he loves it! I can't wait for him to retire and join me as the head of my company's cadre of trainers in our face-to-face

APPENDIX B

workshops for at-risk groups. He will partner with me to maintain high quality standards in the online training programs we develop.

Sean and I have grown our connection with each other in the last five years. Before, we were weathering the storm of Emma's brain injury and prognosis and our dedication to her kept us slogging on. Now, life is smoother, more joyful and free. I love how we are partners in eating healthy and exercising every day. I am lean and strong and pain-free after so many years of the opposite, and I am thankful that I have seen Sean become vibrant and reverse the aging that took place in the first eight years of Emma's brain injury. Tomorrow, we'll jet off for a weekend away together, something we look forward to doing a few times each year. I love this man so much, this man who was willing to sacrifice his own health and sleep to support us all through a challenging decade. I have no doubt that our family was divinely selected to walk this path together.

As I do my daily spiritual work, I think yet again about how far I have come. I've had a life of huge challenges and sometimes it felt like life was trying to beat my spirit into the ground. I worked for decades to dig myself out and climb out of each trench I fell into and my logic took me a long way. My logic helped me to pin down what hurt me and why. It helped me to build scaffolds to climb to another level and stay alive, but my logic could not help me to thrive alone. Thriving began when I started learning about energy work, helping me connect with my intuition, and building a team that was supremely interested in making a difference to those we served. It all helped me feel more supported in my business and, most importantly, in Emma's recovery.

I love running my own business, because starting that gave me a jumpstart when I was almost burned out in heart and mind and spirit. Now I get to light that flame and keep it burning for my own wonderful clients. I'm so thrilled I stepped more fully into being a speaker and author because that filled me up and made me whole. I love being my authentic island-girl self, showing my sense of humour, talking about my simple roots, and sharing my life's journey with others. That's how I help others see themselves for the heroes and changemakers that they are. I love being able to light a spark of hope and inspiration in the hearts and minds of thousands.

Back in my office, my brother and sister knock on my door. They are both thriving too, each in their own heart-centred niches. I love how we are each able to look back on all the pain of our past and see how each low point was preparing us with skills and resilience for this part of our journey. I am glad my mother is able to see the joy we have experienced together, and soon we will have our massive summer vacation with all our families, heading off on a plane to a beach in some wonderful location. (I've finally learned to let go of the reins and stop planning every item on our itinerary; I actually enjoy being surprised and living off the cuff on vacation now!). I feel blessed because our journeys have taught us to love one another even more because of our different personalities and talents as well as our shared valued and strengths.

What a massive change has been wrought in my life in these last five years, I think, as I open my office back door and step into the garden with a cup of tea during my break. I sit on a bench under luscious frangipani flowers and my eyes follow the path traced by the stepping stones scattered across the stretch of lawn. I thrill at the dancing butterflies and hummingbirds loving the flowers' nectar, and chuckle at Emma's laughter floating to me on the breeze. Her wonderful nurse has become a sister to me. I love that woman for every minute she has hoped and prayed and worked beside me to benefit Emma in the last seven years. I look forward to playing with Em later; I look forward to the twinkle in her eyes when she finds my newest garden hiding place.

I'm amazed by how different my life has become as my finances opened up, too. Now, I have no fear about saving enough for the future, contributing to causes that matter to me, investing, building a good home in a nice location, providing for our retirement years (and who plans to retire anyway?) and caring for my employees with amazing compensation packages.

I love that my home is on the beach, and I love the opportunities for physical activity all around us with amenities like a pool and a gym and wonderful big grounds to use as a course if we don't feel like running on the beach sometimes. Best of all, I love the way all the pieces have come together to make a difference to so many people, including my family and me, my friends, my employees and co-workers, and our community of special needs families just like us.

Acknowledgments

To Emma Lucia Priscilla Balkissoon, our daughter: Emma Lou, I am awed by your light and joy each day.

To Bryan: Son, I feel so lucky that even though you are growing up, I can still see your loving heart. Thank you for your regular check-ins to see how I've been managing as I wrote, your constant presence as a friend to Emma, and your partnership with us in caring for her.

To Melissa: Mel, you have not been just a nurse to us. You feel like an extension of our family and I do not take that for granted. Thank you for loving Emma and Bry as though they have two mothers, you and me. Thank you for filling the gaps I can't fill when my own work demands get in the way.

To Sean, especially: You have been the biggest cheerleader of my entire life. You have loved me in the most difficult way there is to love someone—through your constant presence, tireless work to upkeep our family, self-sacrifice, and quiet, abiding strength. I am forever grateful that life led me to you.

I mention in this book how isolated we have often felt since Em's brain injury, but we were blessed that some wonderful people stepped in and stayed close. Love and appreciation for being warm lights in our lives Rakesh, Charmaine and family, Uncle Lloyd, Mickey, Vidia and family, and Aunty Grace. I have been blessed in recent years to meet several wonderful people online, who have become my real-world friends. I am so grateful for every one of you.

Thank you, too, to our immediate families, especially Grandma Polly and Grandpa Harry who call Em every single evening and shore Sean up with their love. Mom and Alice, thanks for going all out with providing beautiful surroundings and forcing me to make an effort for the author photos. Adrian, I can't express how much I value your constant efforts to check in on me and all of us, especially as I've been stretching with this book. I miss Dad at times like this; you light up my life in so many ways that remind me of him.

This book came together at a time when I did not feel I had time or energy to give to any other task, and I credit it to serendipitously having met Lauren Eckhardt Klump, who later became my book coach. Lauren, you gave me the confidence to be vulnerable and shared your family with me, so I felt like a friend and not a distant client. Your critiques, though honest, were never hurtful and always aligned the work better for the reader. To the entire Burning Soul Press team, I appreciate you so much!

I must acknowledge how full my heart has become with every step of writing this book. I have felt connection with so many people for whom I am extremely grateful. I value my forefathers for their resilience and love. I am grateful for those who stayed around long term to embrace us after Em got hurt: you kept us standing when our world was being rocked. I treasure the enthusiasm and support of my Beta readers, not one of whom hesitated when approached to help me critically evaluate and improve the book.

As for those special needs parents and their families for whom this book was written, I have felt an awesome lightness of spirit from somehow feeling the connection of all of our special needs journeys. Friends, I hope that you find something that bolsters you and holds your hand as you wander through these pages.

About the Author

Dr. Marcia Nathai-Balkissoon is a storyteller and educator who believes that we each have a powerful purpose that should guide our lives. As one of her children is brain-injured and bedridden, Marcia and her family have traversed significant challenges. She is passionate about helping special needs families to feel more connected, gain visibility, access and support, and tap into their resilience.

Beyond the special needs context, Marcia helps people connect deeply with their purpose so they can experience more joy and fulfilment. Through intuitive and logical interventions, her work seeks to shift mindsets, build habits, foster creativity and curiosity, and enable people to live their best lives each day, trusting they are enough.

Currently a tenured lecturer at the University of the West Indies, Marcia is most drawn to the fields of health, safety and wellness, business and personal strategy, and teaching and learning. She is a certified Parent Skills Master Trainer and enjoys working with her husband to adapt interventions for their daughter and helping other parents to do the same for their children.

Connect with Marcia and the *Lighting the Path* community:

www.marcianb.com
www.marcianb.com/biolink/

www.ingramcontent.com/pod-product-compliance
Lightning Source LLC
Chambersburg PA
CBHW070044230426
43661CB00005B/754